MIAMI BEACH

CORAL GABLES AND SOUTH MIAMI 102–111

COCONUT GROVE 116–124

If the eyes are the windows to the soul, Miami is the window to *pastelitos*, *coladas* and the good life. Between its amazing year-round weather, its abundant opportunities for recreation and access to the hottest shopping, cuisine, nightlife and people, it is a bon vivant's dream destination. This is the type of place you want to be if you're looking to alternate effortlessly between daily life and vacation – in the office at sunrise and sipping rosé by the ocean at sunset – or, if you're ready for retirement, but you're only in your 30s. It's where you can live large while casually overlooking the fact that you're not rich and famous (yet).

Whether you wish to lounge on a beautiful, white-sand beach, explore the only living coral barrier reef in the US, taste Cuban culture without leaving the country, dance to the beats of world-renowned DJs and musicians, we've got them all. There's a reason Miami is known as The Magic City, and you can only truly understand it after you've been here. I've lived in six different cities and none has invigorated me as much as this has. So put on your sun hat and prepare to have the time of your life!

the hunt miami writer

margarita wells

Margarita Wells moved to Florida from Mexico City at the age of 12, and while she's never stopped pining for the taco paradise where she was born, she fell hard for the palm tree-lined heaven of her adopted city. A marine scientist, Margarita loves Miami's interconnectedness with the sea, its tropical vibes and ability to cater to both a metropolitan beach town and suburban lifestyle. When she's not protecting the local environment, you can find her bumming around her coastal backyard, skateboarding around her neighborhood or checking out the newest hot spots for her blog, thankyoumiami.com.

FREEHAND MIAMI

Hipster stay

2727 Indian Creek Drive (at 28th Street; Miami Beach)
+1 305 531 2727 / thefreehand.com/miami

Double from $90

Freehand Miami merges the affordability and social ambiance of a hostel with the comfort and cleanliness of a hotel – typically mutually exclusive impressions. They primarily offer bunk bed reservations in a shared room that sleeps four or eight, but they also have private quads, private standard king rooms, king suites and bungalows, if you yearn for the privacy of your own space. The perks include free Wi-Fi, bicycle rentals and breakfast. In addition to easy beach access, there's a packed activity calendar – think yoga classes, pool parties and movie nights, as well as some excellent artisanal sips at resident bar The Broken Shaker. Whether you're a local or just visiting, the design, décor and setting are wonderful for a weekend with friends.

MAYFAIR HOTEL & SPA

Luxe sleep

3000 Florida Avenue (at Virginia Street; Coconut Grove)
+1 305 441 0000 / mayfairhotelandspa.com

Double from $150

The high-end Mayfair Hotel & Spa is famous for its amazing rooftop vistas, ample-sized rooms outfitted with soaking tubs and secluded terraces, and its proximity to Coconut Grove's shopping and dining offerings. I'm a fan of the spa's restorative massages – the prices are most reasonable in July and August, when they're offered at a Miami Spa Month discount. My most-loved memory here is of a sunset party during which I alternated expertly between fresh sushi rolls and glasses of prosecco at a cadence reserved for local housewives. But that's what I love about the Mayfair: you don't need to have infinitely deep pockets to treat yourself, especially if you take advantage of their special offers.

ROAM MIAMI

ROAM MIAMI

Extended stay accomodation

118 Southwest South River Drive (near Southwest 1st Street; Little Havana) / +1 305 325 0045 / roammiami.com

Double from $75

I know you're going to love Miami as much as I do, which is why I'm excited my city has a long-stay option so you can really get a feel for local life. This co-living, co-working concept has revitalized the historic Miami River Inn — once the longest continuously operating hotel in the area — to build a gorgeous, temporary subtropical home just for you. For a minimum of a week, you can lease a private suite in one of the property's Old Florida-style bungalows. While you're there, you may find yours truly has become a squatter because I want nothing more than to relax in one of their hammocks, surrounded by their lush landscape, with the promise of a stellar cocktail from restaurant and bar, Casa Florida, on the way.

SENSE BEACH HOUSE

Seaside retreat

400 Ocean Drive (near 4th Street; Miami Beach) / +1 305 538 5529
sensebeachhouse.com

Double from $160

My apartment is on Ocean Drive, which means I share a street with more hotels and restaurants than I do condos. Despite the abundance of venues nearby, I rarely give anything in my immediate vicinity a second look because many are known tourist traps. Sense Beach House is a rare exception. Since it opened in 2012, the 18-room boutique hotel with clean lines and a tranquil ambiance has become a community fixture by regularly hosting pop-ups, yoga classes and other events. Furthermore, their restaurant, The Local House, is all about scrumptious food for a fair value. On the weekends it's usually buzzing with Miamians devoted to their brunch (crab cakes Benny, anyone?), but do note that the midday meal is served daily. Beyond dining, each room has a balcony, plush bedding and posh toiletries. Looking to see what it's like to live as a South Beach local? This is the place for you.

THE BILTMORE

Glam digs

1200 Anastasia Avenue (near De Soto Boulevard; Coral Gables)
+1 855 311 6903 / biltmorehotel.com

Double from $250

Located in the heart of Coral Gables, The Biltmore is an escape from the tourist centers of Miami Beach and Downtown. Its Mediterranean-inspired architecture – implemented by George Merrick in the 1920s – is the pride and joy of the Gables and arguably one of the most gorgeous buildings in town. The rooms are luxe, with high thread count linens, oversized picture windows and seating areas. While I have never been fortunate enough to spend the night here, I frequent it for the famous Sunday brunch – a prix fixe extravaganza of endless caviar, seafood, dessert and mimosas, ideal for celebrating absolutely every special occasion with family and friends. I also love to admire the highly coveted golf course, tennis courts and swimming pool from afar, imagining all of the fantastic times I will enjoy there after I win the lottery.

THE VAGABOND HOTEL

Nostalgia-inspired lodging

7301 Biscayne Boulevard (near Northeast 74th Street; MiMo District)
+1 305 400 8420 / thevagabondhotel.com

Double from $140

The 1950s was a time of artistic creativity that yielded the city's well-known regional style of architecture: Miami Modernist, or MiMo. One of the treasures that still remains from this era is The Vagabond Hotel, a quintessentially Miami venue that was a Rat Pack hangout back in the day. The hotel is known for its unique retro accommodation – think mid-century furnishings in vivid hues and mosaics of mermaids and dolphins – and its restaurant and bar, the latter of which has given the venue a hot spot reputation among foodies. The Vagabond and other nearby MiMo motels have also become go-to backdrops for the sartorial exploits of the fashion blogging set.

THE VAGABOND HOTEL

wynwood

It's hard to remember this city without present-day Wynwood, although I rarely thought of or visited the latter before developer Tony Goldman transformed it into its current, artsy glory. In fact, my first visit to this enclave was during Art Basel in 2010 when my friend Dylan repeatedly insisted we visit the new Wynwood Walls, a place he claimed had must-see street art from international artists like Shepard Fairey and Invader. Eventually, I agreed to go and left the familiarity of my South Beach home for what was, at least for me, the great unknown. A few years and several layers of paint later, the hood's street art has expanded beyond the Wynwood Walls and the community has become the cornerstone of the local art scene.

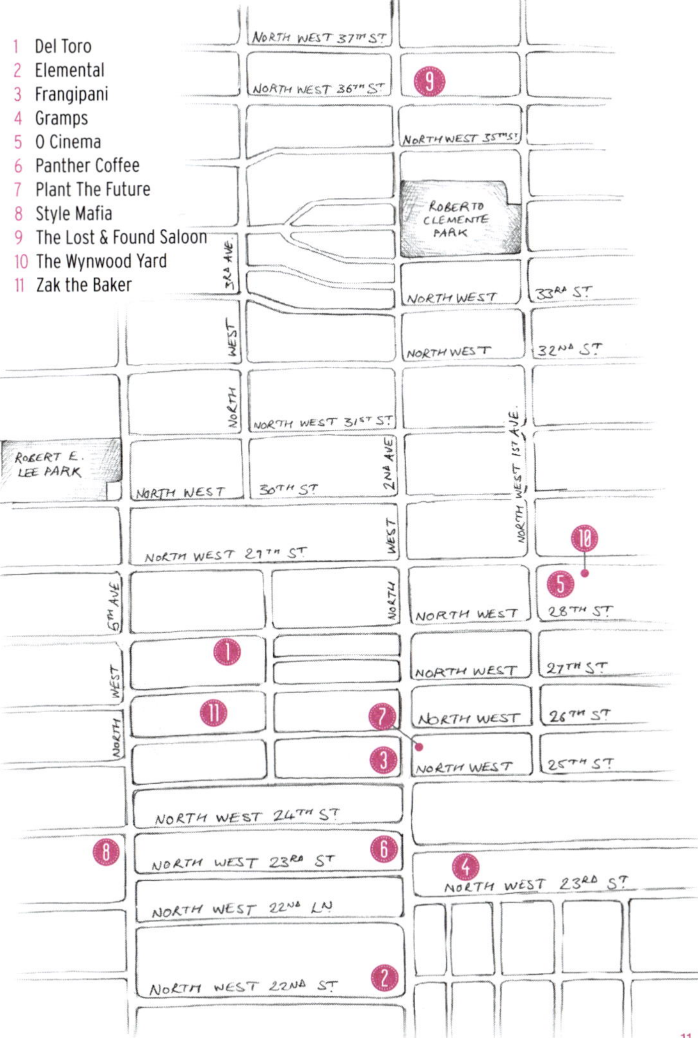

1 Del Toro
2 Elemental
3 Frangipani
4 Gramps
5 O Cinema
6 Panther Coffee
7 Plant The Future
8 Style Mafia
9 The Lost & Found Saloon
10 The Wynwood Yard
11 Zak the Baker
NORTH WEST 37TH ST
NORTH WEST 36TH ST
NORTH WEST 35TH ST
ROBERTO CLEMENTE PARK
NORTH WEST 33RD ST
NORTH WEST 32ND ST
NORTH WEST 31ST ST
NORTH WEST 30TH ST
NORTH WEST 3RD AVE
NORTH WEST 2ND AVE
NORTH WEST 1ST AVE
ROBERT E. LEE PARK
NORTH WEST 29TH ST
NORTH WEST 5TH AVE
NORTH WEST 28TH ST
NORTH WEST 27TH ST
NORTH WEST 26TH ST
NORTH WEST 25TH ST
NORTH WEST 24TH ST
NORTH WEST 23RD ST
NORTH WEST 23RD ST
NORTH WEST 22ND LN
NORTH WEST 22ND ST

DEL TORO

High-end unisex footwear

2750 Northwest 3rd Avenue, Suite 22 (near Northwest 27th Terrace)
+1 305 571 8253 / deltoroshoes.com / Open daily

Most men in South Florida finish college and jump without hesitation into a job in real estate or finance – but not Matthew Chevallard. After graduation, the Italian-born, Palm Beach-raised designer not only identified an opportunity in the shoe market, but leveraged it to start his own company selling chic velvet smoking slippers for men and women. In 10 short years, Del Toro has grown a cult following of fashionistas, Ivy Leaguers and A-list sports stars. The repertoire has also expanded to include other styles such as chukkas, espadrilles, sneakers and Oxfords featuring his smart use of color and stellar Italian craftsmanship, all of which are available at his colorful flagship boutique in Wynwood.

ELEMENTAL

Aesthetic pieces for the home

2399 Northwest 2nd Avenue (at Northwest 24th Street)
+1 786 276 5955 / elementalstore.com / Closed Sunday

You know that envy-inducing house in *Dwell* – the one with the refurbished barn that seemingly perfect couple gutted, remodeled and furnished with amazing mid-century finds from eBay? I dream about it almost every night, but know that it is neither within my means nor my talent to make it possible. That said, I can get reasonably and feasibly close to my ideal abode thanks to Elemental in Wynwood. This shop gives me access to clever works of art, quirky home goods and office gadgets from some of the top product designers in the world so I, too, can bring intrigue into my humble digs.

FRANGIPANI

Inspiring lifestyle boutique

2516 Northwest 2nd Avenue (near Northwest 25th Street)
+1 305 573 1480 / frangipanimiami.com / Open daily

Sometimes I wish I had some sort of gift-o-matic closet, where every time I'd walk in looking for the ideal baby shower or housewarming gift, I'd come right out with something that totally suits the recipient. Enter Frangipani, home to an array of awesome objects and the kind of place where I end up taking a couple of laps to make sure I didn't miss anything. What I also love about Frangipani is its playful setup, where porcelain tableware is displayed next to lomo cameras and colorful board shorts from local brand Algae. The focus here is on showcasing how well-designed, sustainable goods can add excitement to the day-to-day. And, excited is exactly how I leave after every visit.

GRAMPS

Laid-back bar with live music

176 Northwest 24th Street (near Northwest 2nd Avenue)
+1 305 699 2669 / gramps.com / Open daily

My favorite evenings are spent outside, accompanied by a killer soundtrack, an excellent setting and fabulous company. Gramps, with its outdoor terrace replete with picnic tables and its consistently solid programming, meets two out of the three criteria right off the bat. For these reasons, it's become one of the emergency spots in my repertoire for those times when I need to let off some steam or to salvage a less-than-perfect day. In fact, Gramps is the kind of place I'd recommend to friends for a first date because the hubbub of their trivia nights, bingo sessions and themed, monthly parties offers a nice distraction during any unanticipated awkward moments.

O CINEMA

Community movie theater

90 Northwest 29th Street (at Northwest 1st Avenue)
+1 305 571 9970 / wynwood.o-cinema.org / Open daily

Since I started blogging, I've been exposed to more and more of the city's rare creative types, the kind that went to art and film school and would be better suited for New York or L.A. but decided (thankfully) to keep their talents here. It's because of two of them, fashion bloggers Angeles Almuna and Jana Carrero, that I first set foot in O Cinema. The independent, single-screen venue shows all genres, from art to foreign to cult classics. Not coincidentally, my first visit was for the screening of a feature starring Angeles and Jana – it's exactly this support of the homegrown artistic community that makes O Cinema so special.

PANTHER COFFEE

Serious bean roasters

2390 Northwest 2nd Avenue (at Northwest 24th Street)
+1 305 677 3952 / panthercoffee.com / Open daily

As a self-proclaimed java addict-slash-snob, I take my brew very seriously. When I travel, I force my companions to venture from one specialty coffee shop to another as I get my caffeine fix, analyze the differences in each beverage and get a feel for the local flair. After all, I have been known to claim that cafés are microcosms of their surrounding communities, a saying that originated from my observations of what each Panther Coffee outpost says about its area. While I am partial to the Sunset Harbour outlet, the Wynwood location holds a special place in my heart because it's the original and a hub for the neighborhood's start-up and artsy folks. The coffee menu is overwhelmingly large, but you can't go wrong with an almond milk latte, a cortadito (a Cuban espresso) or a cold brew.

PLANT THE FUTURE

Forward-thinking florist

2511 Northwest 2nd Avenue (near Northwest 25th Street)
+1 305 571 7177 / plantthefuture.com / Open daily

I am a huge believer in biophilia, the idea that there is an instinctive bond between humans and other living systems. There are few things that can cheer me up like the natural energy of a fresh bouquet or a bonsai garden. Therein lies the magic of Paloma Teppa's garden-inspired designs, which, since the opening of her shop in Wynwood, have taken over Miami in the form of living walls and foliage-accessorized sculptures around town. The minute you enter her store, you will find it hard not to be swept away by the surreal creations of her floating terrariums and colorful plant-based art, which will make you feel like you're simultaneously entering another planet and being further grounded to Earth.

STYLE MAFIA

Sartorial finds

2324 Northwest 5th Avenue (near Northwest 24th Street)
+1 786 801 0319 / stylemafia.us / Closed Sunday

If you want proof that The Magic City breeds talent, look no further than Simonett Pereira, who launched her first clothing collection when she was only 22. These days, her showroom sees a rotating clientele of fashion "It girls" looking for affordable luxury to bridge, as Simonett calls it, "the gap between their social life and their income level". What I love are the original, trendy pieces that she dreams up season after season. Think voluminous tops with billowy (and extra long) sleeves as well as outrageously flared trousers – half of which I want to wear, the other half of which I wish I knew how to wear. And that's part of the appeal of Style Mafia's designs.

THE LOST & FOUND SALOON

Tex-Mex bites and craft beer

185 Northwest 36th Street (near Northwest 2nd Avenue)
+1 305 576 1008 / thelostandfoundsaloon-miami.com / Open daily

Amid trendy cafés and art galleries, a western bar was the last thing I expected to find in Wynwood. Nevertheless, The Lost & Found Saloon has managed to stand its ground by offering nosh for everyone. There is a wide range of vegetarian and vegan options that seem out of place for a joint decorated in cowhides and bourbon bottles, but I can vouch for those dishes as my friend Sam regularly raves about them. He absolutely loves the Posse Energy Burrito – filled with saffron rice, refried beans, Manchego, cheddar, Montery Jack cheese, lettuce and tomato – which he declares "the yummiest in all of Miami". For me, the appeal lies in the kitschy, eye-catching décor and extensive collection of hot sauces.

RECOMMENDED BY
ASHLEY BROZIC
FREELANCE WRITER

THE WYNWOOD YARD

Culinary and cultural incubator

56 Northwest 29th Street (near Northwest 1st Avenue)
+1 305 771 4810 / thewynwoodyard.com / Closed Monday

Over the past few years, Miami has become a center of entrepreneurial activity at both a grassroots and more corporate level. Newest to the party is The Wynwood Yard, which is bringing food-centric events such as farmers markets, concerts and networking happy hours to a vibrant outdoor space in the heart of the enclave. Beyond the roster of gourmet vendors, my favorite part about this concept is that it was an initiative started by a talented group of young business and F&B professionals who continue to serve as mentors to the community they have created. It's places like this that are building and securing a prosperous future for this city.

ZAK THE BAKER

Kosher bakery and café

405 Northwest 26th Street
(near Northwest 3rd Avenue)
+1 786 347 7100 / zakthebaker.com
Closed Saturday

I'm a fan of a simple yet enjoyable meal prepared with quality ingredients, which is probably why I'm obsessed with everything that Zak Stern makes. The first time I tried his famous bread was at a market, where I picked up a cranberry walnut loaf to bring home. As I was leaving, I ripped off a piece, chewing through its coarse crust and savoring its freshness. By the time I was back in my car, the entire thing was gone. Since then, his loaves – arguably the finest in town – have become my staple. While it is a pleasant surprise to find his naturally leavened offerings in restaurants and grocery stores throughout the city, nowhere is it more scrumptious than when it is fresh out of the oven of this Wynwood gem.

culture vulture

A peek into our art and culture hot spots

LITTLE HAITI CULTURAL CENTER
212 Northeast 59th Terrace (near Northeast 2nd Avenue; Little Haiti), +1 305 960 2969
littlehaiticulturalcenter.com, closed Monday

LOWE ART MUSEUM
1301 Stanford Drive (near George E. Merrick Drive; Coral Gables), +1 305 284 3535
lowemuseum.org, closed Monday

PÉREZ ART MUSEUM MIAMI
1103 Biscayne Boulevard (near Museum Drive; Downtown), +1 305 375 3000
pamm.org, closed Wednesday

RUBELL FAMILY COLLECTION
95 Northwest 29th Street (at Northwest 1st Avenue; Wynwood), +1 305 573 6090, rfc.museum
open Wednesday through Saturday

THE WOLFSONIAN-FLORIDA INTERNATIONAL UNIVERSITY
1001 Washington Avenue (at 10th Street; Miami Beach), +1 305 531 1001, wolfsonian.org
closed Wednesday

Miami is known as the "Gateway to the Americas" and rightfully so. The majority of our foreign-born nationals (myself included) hail from Latin America and the Caribbean, and The Magic City's location makes it easy to get here. The constant influx of new residents from these countries has been the primary driving force in shaping Miami's arts and culture scene. I brought with me influences from Mexico that I've incorporated into my life here and similarly, expats from other countries have carried their traditions over. For example, the **Little Haiti Cultural Center** brings the sights, sounds (and sometimes tastes) of Haiti to locals and visitors through exhibitions like *The More I Let Go, The More I Am Home: A Visual Memoir*, which showed recently and celebrated Haitian-American women artists, as well as open-mic nights and arts, dance and language classes.

PÉREZ ART MUSEUM MIAMI

That said, the effects that shape the arts scene extend beyond geographical customs. The community is also made up of prominent individuals who are able to bring incredible opportunities to town. Wynwood holds one of the world's largest curation of privately owned contemporary art thanks to the **Rubell Family Collection**, which houses the works of over 800 artists, such as heavy-hitters Jean-Michel Basquait, Keith Haring, Jeff Koons, Yayoi Kusama and Kara Walker in its 28-gallery museum.

Downtown, **Pérez Art Museum Miami** – a partnership between the Miami-Dade County and the Miami Art Museum of Dade County Association, Inc. – is home to international modern art from the 20th and 21st centuries, due in part to donations from notable figures like real estate mogul and author Jorge M. Pérez. The collection includes pieces from Diego Rivera, Purvis Young, Beatriz González, Kiki Smith, and Joaquín Torres-García.

The city's universities have also gotten in on the artsy action. **The Wolfsonian-Florida International University** alone boasts approximately 180,000 pieces of furniture, industrial-design objects and a variety of other media from the 1850s to the 1950s. These can be found on display at its Miami Beach location to incite discussion on how design has shaped the world. Not to be outdone, the University of Miami's (Go 'Canes!) **Lowe Art Museum** features impressive Egyptian, Roman and Greek antiquities. But, most importantly, they have found the key to draw the younger generations closer to our unexpectedly robust cultural gems: after-hours exhibits prefaced with a cocktail reception. Cheers to that!

THE WOLFSONIAN-FLORIDA INTERNATIONAL UNIVERSITY

miami design district

little haiti

One of this city's superpowers is its ability to seamlessly marry dichotomous realities under one identity. For example, the ultra-luxurious Miami Design District, known for its offerings in high-end art, fashion and restaurants, coexists – for better or worse – with its culturally rich, but money-poor neighbor, Little Haiti. Streets lined with boutiques of international brand royalty, including Chanel, Cartier and Dior, give way to warehouses featuring music studios and dive bars that welcome you with a reminder not to leave valuables in your car because they will most likely be gone before you return. But no matter how economically different these two communities may be, each has a lot to offer (in their own way) in terms of food, shopping and culture, making them typically Miami.

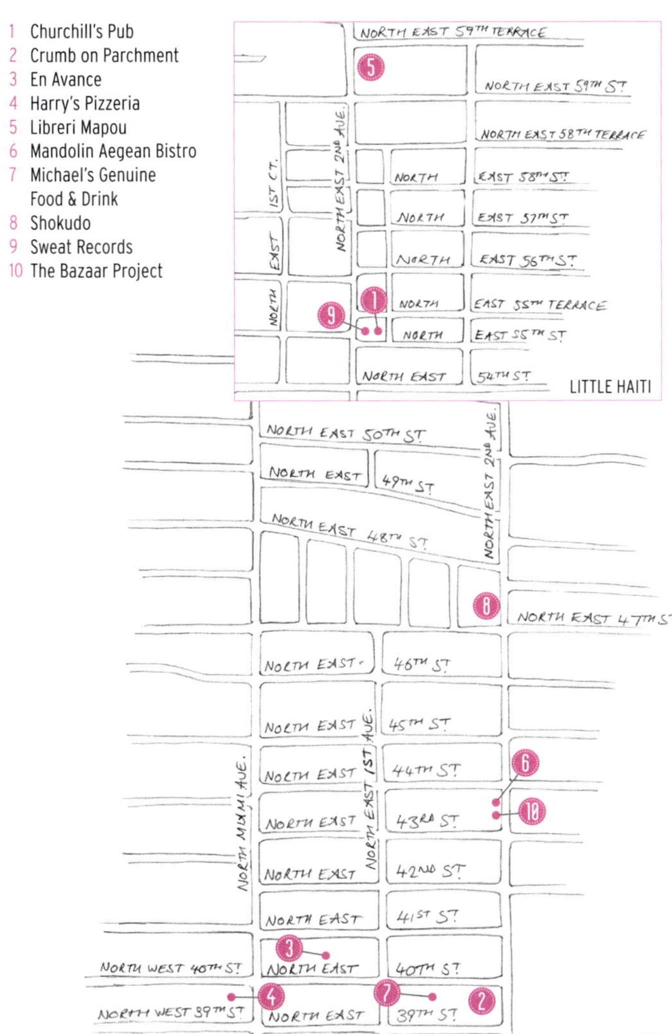

1 Churchill's Pub
2 Crumb on Parchment
3 En Avance
4 Harry's Pizzeria
5 Libreri Mapou
6 Mandolin Aegean Bistro
7 Michael's Genuine Food & Drink
8 Shokudo
9 Sweat Records
10 The Bazaar Project
NORTH EAST 59TH TERRACE
NORTH EAST 59TH ST
NORTH EAST 58TH TERRACE
NORTH EAST 58TH ST
NORTH EAST 57TH ST
NORTH EAST 56TH ST
NORTH EAST 55TH TERRACE
NORTH EAST 55TH ST
NORTH EAST 54TH ST
NORTH EAST 1ST CT.
NORTH EAST 2ND AVE.
LITTLE HAITI
NORTH EAST 50TH ST
NORTH EAST 49TH ST
NORTH EAST 48TH ST
NORTH EAST 47TH ST
NORTH EAST 46TH ST
NORTH EAST 45TH ST
NORTH EAST 44TH ST
NORTH EAST 43RD ST
NORTH EAST 42ND ST
NORTH EAST 41ST ST
NORTH EAST 40TH ST
NORTH EAST 39TH ST
NORTH WEST 40TH ST
NORTH WEST 39TH ST
NORTH MIAMI AVE.
NORTH EAST 1ST AVE.

CHURCHILL'S PUB

Dive bar with live rock, punk and jazz

5501 Northeast 2nd Avenue (at Northeast 55th Street)
+1 305 757 1807 / churchillspub.com / Open daily

In a city with many dining options and high rents, many venues here close nearly as soon as they open. Because of that, there are few places that have been around long enough to be considered iconic. Churchill's is the one – if not the only – exception to this rule, making enough of an impression to be dubbed Miami's version of New York's dearly departed CBGB by some. The establishment, founded by British entertainment promoter Dave Daniels, opened in Little Haiti in 1979 and has been serving live music for so many years that it's practically a rite of passage to see a concert here.

CRUMB ON PARCHMENT

Hidden, dainty café

3930 Northeast 2nd Avenue (near Northeast 40th Street)
+1 305 572 9444 / facebook.com/CrumbMiami
Closed Saturday and Sunday

When I first stepped into the atrium of The Melin Building, the last thing I expected to find was a replica of a Cape Cod-style living room. Yet there it sits prettily, amidst shops like Ornare and Adriana Hoyos, looking as cozy and inviting as ever. Maybe it's the décor, maybe it's the menu – with coffees, teas, soups, salads, sandwiches and pastries – but this is the place I go to let my inner debutante out and pretend I'm having high tea or luncheon. I love kale salads, and highly recommend chef Michelle Bernstein's super refreshing version, which helps me feel better about mindlessly indulging in the bakery's mouthwatering quiches and confections. After all, a balanced diet is a doughnut in each hand, right?

EN AVANCE

Upscale boutique showcasing global brands

53 Northeast 40th Street (near Northeast 1st Avenue)
+1 305 576 0056 / enavance.co / Closed Sunday (except during Fall)

I've always wondered whether Karen Quinones named her store En Avance (French for "in advance") as a nod to the fashion-forward clothes she sells or her ability to find retail real estate gold well before it develops into major shopping destinations. Prior to settling into its current space, En Avance was a Lincoln Road Mall pioneer. Then in 2008, the establishment was one of the first to move into the Miami Design District, amid warehouses and stores dedicated solely to furniture and home décor. Today, she shares walls with some of the biggest names in fashion. But Quinones has found her niche in scouting the market to fill her shop with under-the-radar clothing and jewelry lines that set her apart from her high-profile neighbors.

HARRY'S PIZZERIA

Fabulous wood-fired oven treats

3918 North Miami Avenue (near Northwest 39th Street)
+1 786 275 4963 / harryspizzeria.com / Open daily

For me, the term "neighborhood pizza place" evokes memories of greasy cardboard boxes stacked on a kitchen counter, but when it comes to Harry's Pizzeria, that imagery couldn't be further from reality. The cozy spot owned by chef Michael Schwartz has been redefining the homegrown pizza joint concept since 2011 by keeping the friendly service but elevating the experience and the standard recipe. The menu is composed of 10 mouthwatering variations and one daily special; my default is the rock shrimp option, which is available every day. I didn't expect to find grilled lemon embedded under the top layer of Manchego the first time I tried it, but it turned out to be an absolutely winning combination I have repeated during subsequent visits, and highly recommend.

LIBRERI MAPOU

Literary and cultural center

5919 Northeast 2nd Avenue
(near Northeast 59th Terrace)
+1 305 757 9922
facebook.com/librerimapou
Closed Thursday

As a Mexican immigrant, I understand the importance of keeping the heritage of my birth country alive and mixing it with my new American identity. Haitian author, playwright, director and arts advocate Jan Mapou does, too. When he moved here in the late '80s, he wanted to be the spark that kept Haitian culture alive. To that end, Mapou started by distributing his extensive collection of Caribbean-inspired reading materials in French, English and Creole. He has since grown what has been dubbed the "Best Haitian Bookstore in Miami" by local media into a hotbed of culture, with an impressive display of his private art collection and lauded exhibitions of Haitian works.

MANDOLIN AEGEAN BISTRO

Chic Greek restaurant with al fresco dining

4312 Northeast 2nd Avenue (near Northeast 43rd Street)
+1 305 749 9140 / mandolinmiami.com / Open daily

Despite being a coastal city, Miami doesn't really offer the romantic beach-town setting for which places like Mykonos and Santorini are known. It's just not our forte. Nevertheless, this hidden find has done a fantastic job of bringing some of that Mediterranean flair here, both in its ambiance and cuisine. Owners Anastasia and Ahmet transformed this space into a gorgeous candlelit courtyard, nestled between two white-and-blue houses reminiscent of Greece's seaside towns. Then, drawing from their Greek and Turkish backgrounds, they buillt upon the setting with dishes like grilled octopus and lamb ribs so tasty my friend Jamison and I fought for every bite during our most recent visit.

SHOKUDO

Asian nosh

4740 Northeast 2nd Avenue (near Northeast 48th Street)
+1 305 758 7782 / shokudomiami.com / Open daily

Growing up in Mexico City instilled in me a deep appreciation for street food. I find that there's something about the questionable cleanliness of the whole process that makes the fare taste extra delicious. But, not everyone's stomach can handle eating such grub and – let's face it – it's often not worth the risk of getting sick. For those of you who have more sensitive stomachs (and perhaps sensibilities), Shokudo is a clean outpost for trying Asian street eats. Owner Yoko Takarada favors the classic preparation of Eastern dishes over the cliché Asian fusion. The can't-miss dishes on the menu are chef Armando Litiatco's miso ramen, Korean kalbi ribs and Thai yum woon sen (spicy glass noodles).

SWEAT RECORDS

Vinyl store and concert hall

5505 Northeast 2nd Avenue (near Northeast 55th Street)
+1 786 693 9309 / sweatrecordsmiami.com / Open daily

The city's live music scene has long been hindered by the fact that we're located at the southern tip of a long state. Yes, we get Top 40 artists who fly in on private jets to perform sold-out concerts at the AmericanAirlines Arena, but smaller bands who travel in tour buses and couchsurf their way across the country rarely make it our way due to time and financial constraints. Tired of being left out of the indie scene, friends Lauren "Lolo" Reskin and Sara Yousuf, who met working at a college radio station, decided to take matters into their own hands and opened Sweat Records behind Churchill's Pub (see pg 30) in 2005. Since then, it has established itself as the go-to venue to watch bands perform and discover hard-to-find albums.

THE BAZAAR PROJECT

Gorgeous picks

4308 Northeast 2nd Avenue (at Northeast 43rd Street)
+1 786 703 6153 / thebazaarproject.com / Open daily

When I win the Powerball, my first order of business will be to pack my bags and take off on a trip around the world so I can see new places, experience other cultures and collect exotic trinkets that remind me of my travels. Until then, I'm enjoying life here with my fingers crossed and investing my moderate budget on one-off pieces that reflect my inner jetsetter. One of my favored venues to shop is The Bazaar Project, an intimate boutique that stocks handcrafted jewelry and housewares sourced from all over the world. Whether I'm looking for a gift for a friend or for myself, the originality and beauty of its inventory have made this place a well-loved one.

mimo district

biscayne corridor

Driving along Biscayne Boulevard is a bit like time traveling. The trip through this north-south corridor is peppered with architectural gems from times past, like the Freedom Tower from the 1920s and The Bacardi Building from the 1960s amidst the skyline's newer high-rises. The MiMo District, generally bound between 50th and 77th Streets, is particularly fun to traverse, if only to take a peek at the 1950s motels that still remain in the area. While some of these buildings, such as the South Pacific Motel, have been abandoned and are seriously run-down, others – like The Vagabond Motel (see pg 9) – have been transformed into hot spots that revel in their MiMo glory. Slowly but surely, more developers are shining the spotlight here, and businesses – particularly some of the city's most adored restaurant concepts – are choosing to call this area home.

1 Blue Collar
2 C. Madeleine's (off map)
3 Fly Boutique
4 LetterHeads
5 Ms. Cheezious
6 Ni.Do. Caffé
7 The Consignment Bar

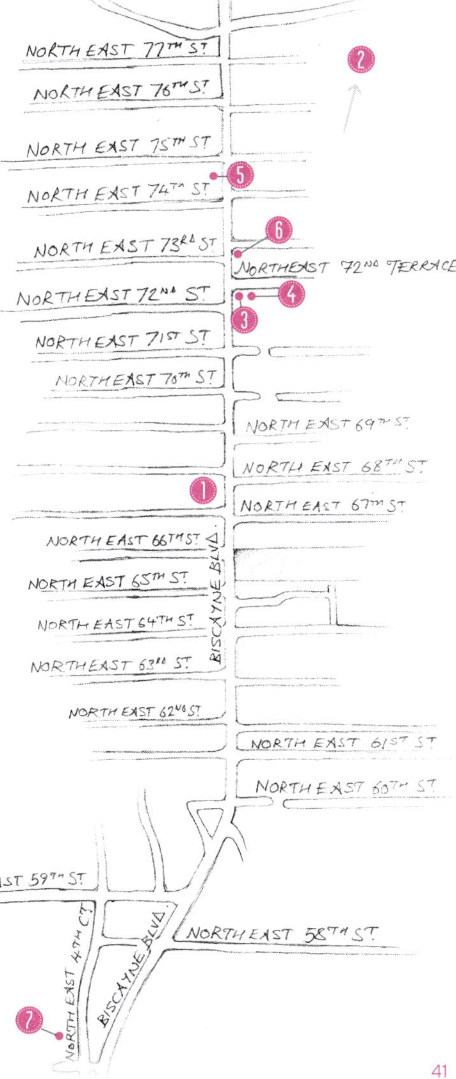

BLUE COLLAR

Hearty eats

6730 Biscayne Boulevard (near Northeast 68th Street)
+1 305 756 0366 / bluecollarmiami.com / Open daily

Blue Collar has gained a cult following since opening in 2012. Chef and owner Daniel Serfer's success comes as no surprise, as this young native knows what hungry locals want. The portions are generous, the food is excellent and every little detail adds to its diner ambiance. We're talking about coffee served in an old-school Thermos and milk served in a glass jar. Plus, there is a je ne sais quoi perpetuated by Serfer's nods to his hometown amidst a menu of comfort fare. I'm particularly intrigued by the Corbencito, a braised brisket sandwich on a Portuguese muffin with a side of latkes named after local documentary filmmaker and Blue Collar regular, Billy Corben.

C. MADELEINE'S

Celeb-worthy, pre-loved designer threads

13702 Biscayne Boulevard (near Highlands Drive)
+1 305 945 7770 / cmadeleines.com / Open daily

Famed fashion photographer Bruce Weber loves Miami as much as he loves his ever-present bandana. He frequents Heat games, adores Little Haiti and has shot iconic magazine editorials inspired by The Magic City, including a 2008 *W Magazine* spread entitled "Summer Camp" featuring C. Madeleine's. The shoot's behind-the-scenes video deftly captures the glamour and appeal of this vintage mecca. Every time I see it, I watch in wonder as some of my sartorial icons, including Alexander Wang, Kate Moss and Sasha Pivovarova scour the store's extensive racks of goods from the 1930s to 1990s, trying on everything from furs and gowns to sequined capes. Who would've thought Weber and Moss's discerning fashion tastes would find their match in my city – next to a strip mall, no less? The other thing I love about this shop is that once a year (usually in June or July), the entire inventory goes on sale.

FLY BOUTIQUE

Retro finds

7235 Biscayne Boulevard (at Northeast 72nd Terrace)
+1 305 604 8508 / flyboutiquevintage.com / Closed Saturday

In a time when street style is as important as the clothes making their debut on the runway, leaving the house can be an extremely daunting experience – at least for a fashionista like me. A great ensemble boosts my confidence, improves my mood and sets the tone for my day, so I depend on original, flattering pieces to spice up my look when it needs a little oomph. Fly Boutique is a shop of unexpected sartorial hits in the form of '70s band T-shirts, Americana belts, blingy handbags and gowns of yesteryear – exactly the type of place I visit to stock up on those one-of-a-kind statement pieces.

LETTERHEADS

Delightful letterpressed paper goods

600 Northeast 72nd Terrace (near Biscayne Boulevard)
+1 305 751 4894 / letterheadsmiami.com / Closed Sunday and Monday

There's something utterly special about receiving snail mail these days, especially when our interactions with others are primarily digital, and LetterHeads is helping to keep the art of old-fashioned communication alive with an almost endless array of writing materials. I could spend hours ogling the Instagram-worthy fonts and colors of their party invitations, holiday cards and custom stationery. Plus, owners Maria and Marilynn make the visit to their studio a truly enjoyable experience by tailoring their service to your needs and going above and beyond to deliver. Whether you're just looking for a cute note to say thank you or a bespoke invite, you can bet your bottom dollar LetterHeads has got your back.

MS. CHEEZIOUS

Melty, grilled cheese goodness

7418 Biscayne Boulevard
(near Northeast 74th Street)
+1 305 989 4019 / mscheezious.com
Open daily

The local culinary scene is ever-changing and can be difficult to follow. This makes Ms. Cheezious a homegrown miracle. The first time I heard about it was in 2010, when the three partners – Brian and Fatima Mullins, and M. Christian Dickens – started a food truck feeding the masses at big cultural events like Art Basel and Wynwood Art Walk, and consistently had long lines. These days, they've expanded to two food trucks and two successful brick and mortar locations, starting with this one in the MiMo District, which I depend on for my fix of goat cheese and prosciutto on rye, and crabby cheese and barbecued pulled pork melts.

NI.DO. CAFFÉ

Unpretentious Italian eatery

7295 Biscayne Boulevard (at Northeast 73rd Street)
+1 305 960 7022 / nidocaffe.com / Open daily

I love that the district's choice places to dine at are often in the most modest locations. Ni.Do. Caffé is the perfect example. I found this laid-back venue tucked away in an unassuming shopping center off Biscayne Boulevard after a failed trip to the Japanese market on the 79th Street Causeway. My friend and I had reached record "hangry" levels after a one-hour wait at the tiny and crowded sushi counter, so we decided to eat elsewhere. That's how we ended up here, savoring some of the most delectable paccheri and lasagna we'd ever had. In addition to delish homemade food, there's a beautiful space with outdoor seating that's ideal for sipping wine and nibbling on charcuterie when I'm looking for a break from my South Beach happy hour routine.

THE CONSIGNMENT BAR

Fashion resale

5580 Northeast 4th Court, Suite 4A (near Northeast 56th Street)
+1 305 751 9996 / consignmentbar.com / Closed Monday

There's no subtle way to put it – I enjoy the finer things in life, but have to find ingenious ways to satisfy my tastes without breaking the bank. While some people take water cooler breaks, I make time throughout the day to peruse new inventory on Poshmark and Hautelook, hunting for designer bargains I simply couldn't afford at retail price. My best friend and I spend our weekends in thrift stores, playing tug-of-war over that YSL blouse we both want. When we're feeling particularly diva-like, we head to The Consignment Bar because owner CC Levin takes the "ick" factor out of shopping for pre-owned luxury goods. If you're on a budget but picky, you just can't beat this shop – the inventory looks practically new.

Eat Outdoors

Choice spots for al fresco dining

ANTICA MARE
7999 Northeast Bayshore Court (at Northeast 80th Street; Shorecrest), +1 305 398 1001, anticamare.com closed Monday

CASABLANCA SEAFOOD BAR & GRILL
400 Northwest North River Drive (at Northwest 4th Street; Downtown), +1 305 371 4107 casablancaseafood.com, open daily

OLA
1745 James Avenue (near 18th Street, Miami Beach) +1 305 695 9125, olamiami.com, open daily

PEACOCK GARDEN CAFE
2889 McFarlane Road (near South Bayshore Drive; Coconut Grove), +1 305 774 3332 jaguarhg.com/peacockspot, open daily

SOYKA
5556 Northeast 4th Court (near Northeast 55th Terrace; MiMo District), +1 305 759 3117 soykarestaurant.com, open daily

THE BUTCHER SHOP BEER GARDEN & GRILL
165 Northwest 23rd Street (near Northwest 1st Court; Wynwood), +1 305 846 9120 thebutchershopmiami.com, open daily

PEACOCK GARDEN CAFE

THE BUTCHER SHOP BEER GARDEN & GRILL

When I ask visitors what they love about this city, the answer is almost always "the beautiful climate". Similarly, all of the guests I've hosted have requested to go to a restaurant where they can dine outdoors and bask in the glorious weather. So I can be a good hostess (and for my own enjoyment), I've refined my list of places that offer excellent outdoor dining experiences. Some have the added benefit of being waterfront, but all have consistently stellar menus and give diners access to the city's balmy weather.

Casablanca Seafood Bar & Grill is a fantastic example of tried-and-true seafood fare along the Miami River. My friends and I have been lucky to sit waterside on their dock on every visit, which makes the experience here lovelier.

Similarly, Italian restaurant **Antica Mare**'s covered terrace is a fab place to be at sunset when you get a killer view of the colorful evening sky over Biscayne Bay, complemented by a well-executed menu of Tuscan specialties. As a tuna addict, I can't say no to their tuna sashimi with truffle carpaccio, which is lip-smackingly

decadent without being over-the-top. Surprisingly, my other choice dish is their oven-roasted chicken breast, which may sound boring but comes with the crispiest skin I've ever tasted.

It's not all about the sea views though. South Beach's Sanctuary Hotel is off-the-beaten-path and an oasis primed for enjoying the Latin American fusion menu of its restaurant, **Ola** – particularly their smoked marlin tacos and cheese bread.

In Coconut Grove, the elegant **Peacock Garden Cafe** features a verdant terrace that makes me feel like I'm dining in the midst of a tropical rainforest. Likewise, **The Butcher Shop Beer Garden & Grill** in Wynwood and **Soyka** in the MiMo District have the ability to whisk you away to another place: a German biergarten and a European alley, respectively. Most importantly, they all offer the option of sitting outdoors and savoring the wonderful atmosphere. Isn't that the main reason you're here in the first place?

SOYKA

miami beach

Disclaimer: this hood is my home base. It's important you know that right off the bat because "beach people," as the "mainlanders" call us, are infamous for our bias toward our barrier island community and, subsequently, for rarely leaving "the Beach". But, c'mon, can you blame us? We live in one of the most stunning areas the city has to offer and (almost) everything we want or need is on our island. The minute you drive east over the causeway, windows down, music blaring and saltwater in the air, you'll get exactly what I mean. Miami Beach elicits in me a constant state of euphoria – whether I'm in South Beach with its quirkiness and party vibes, in Middle Beach with its old glamour or in North Beach amidst its ongoing revitalization. In only seven square miles, we've managed to fit it all: beaches, parks, hotels, restaurants, museums, shops and nightclubs. If, like me, you're looking for the complete package, this is the neighborhood for you.

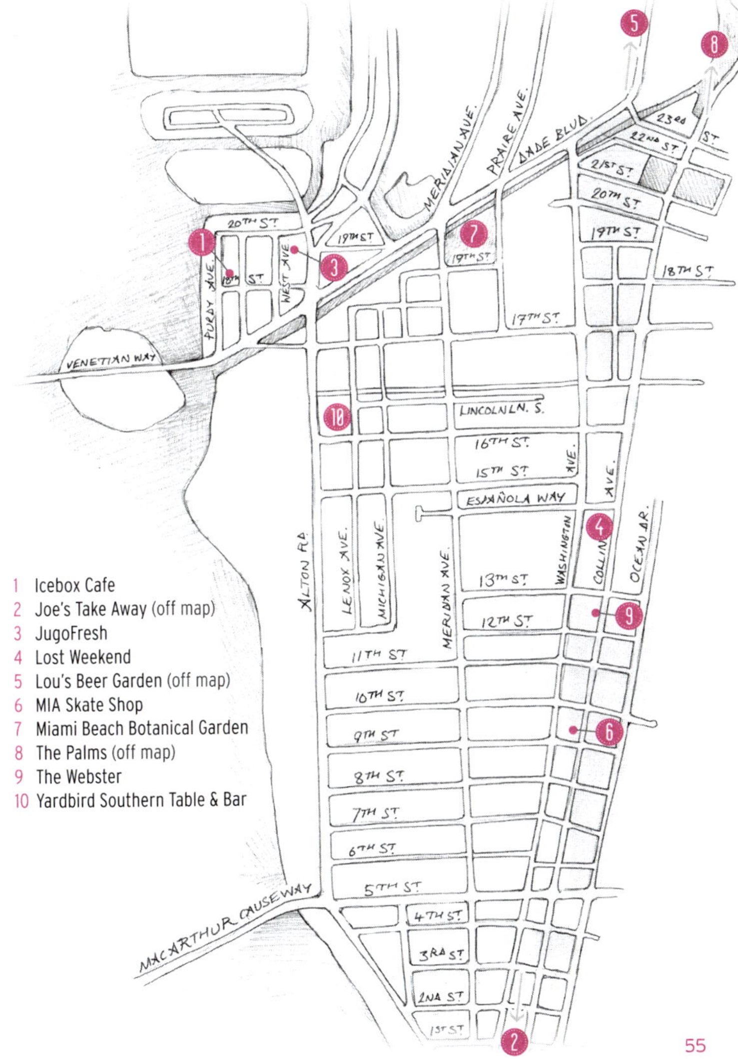

1 Icebox Cafe
2 Joe's Take Away (off map)
3 JugoFresh
4 Lost Weekend
5 Lou's Beer Garden (off map)
6 MIA Skate Shop
7 Miami Beach Botanical Garden
8 The Palms (off map)
9 The Webster
10 Yardbird Southern Table & Bar

ICEBOX CAFE

Oprah-endorsed deliciousness

1855 Purdy Avenue (near 18th Street)
+1 305 538 8448 / iceboxcafe.com
Open daily

There are a few places in this town that thrive without being too new, too classic or too hip in that ironic way. Icebox Cafe is one of them – it just hangs beneath the Sunset Harbour Garage breezeway in its understated coolness. Sure, Oprah once claimed her most-loved dessert was their dark chocolate cake with its layers of cheesecake brownie and chocolate mousse filling, but even then it never got that line-out-the-door attention. I personally prefer it that way because their menu is one of my absolute favorites, be it lunch, dinner or brunch. I've celebrated birthdays, held business meetings and even toasted the end of a yoga class here, searching for any excuse to enjoy their Thai-style coconut soup, avocado and seed salad, and salmon burger.

JOE'S TAKE AWAY

Must-try seafood experience

11 Washington Avenue (near South Pointe Drive) / +1 305 673 4611
joesstonecrab.com / Open daily (October to May)

As much as I love this city's trendy food scene, nothing beats a plastic container of medium stone crab claws, a lobster roll and fried chicken from Joe's Take Away. The cafeteria-style neighbor to renowned Joe's Stone Crab is the go-to alternative for curing a Joe's fix when you don't want to make a reservation, dress up and wait for over an hour to eat. Here, you can order at the register, snag a free table, wait for your number to be called and happily dig into your food within 10 to 15 minutes. If the line is long – which it often is – look for a spot at the bar where you can be served by the bartender. Unfortunately, both Joe's are only open during stone crab season (October to May), so get it in while it's open.

JUGOFRESH

Health nut hangout

1935 West Avenue, Suite 102 (at 20th Street) / +1 786 472 2552
jugofresh.com / Open daily

Calling all raw foodies, nutrition fanatics and party animals looking to detox after a long weekend. Jugofresh is what you want. Aside from uber-healthy options like açaí bowls and oatmeal with goji berries, there's a juice or smoothie for your every want, need or ailment. My friend Betsy and I swear by their saca lo shots, which we take before and after every flight, on days when we are sleep deprived and when a cold is going around our office. The combination of ginger, turmeric, echinacea extract, citrus and other good-for-you ingredients is super spicy, but once you get it down, you can feel it instantly kicking your immune system into high gear. They are always coming up with new recipes using fresh, organic produce. I can't wait to see what's next.

LOST WEEKEND

Dive bar for Miamians

218 Española Way (at Collins Court) / +1 305 672 1707
sub-culture.org / Open daily

South Beach's social scene is all about juxtaposition. You're either into the excess and hubbub of its lounges and clubs, or the casual cool of its dives. When I moved here, I went through a clubbing phase until my friends cajoled me into a night at Lost Weekend and I had an incredible time. The experience made me realize I prefer a relaxed, down-to-earth atmosphere, and would much rather dress in a T-shirt, jeans and boots than a bandage dress. Since then, Lost Weekend has become my choice for a night on the town, especially when I'm planning to be out for a while or with a large party. The sprawling space lets our group spread out and play pool, and when we're looking to nibble, we usually order bar bites from resident restaurant, The Alibi, one of the area's best-kept secrets.

LOU'S BEER GARDEN

Where everybody knows your name

7337 Harding Avenue (near 74th Street) / +1 305 704 7879
lousbeergarden.com / Open daily

When I'm here, I feel like I'm on the set of some '90s movie, where the characters around me share a complicated romantic history replete with tension, but still manage to hang out. Maybe it's the throwback music or the fact that I'm sitting by the pool of an old Miami Beach condo that makes it seem like a backdrop for a dating drama. Or perhaps it's the prime people-watching or the cast of locals, most of whom are regulars you start to recognize after a while. Whether you want to daydream like me or relax outdoors with a cold pint and a juicy burger, the chill ambiance of this insider venue is fantastic.

MIA SKATE SHOP

Hipster skate retailer

229 9th Street (near Collins Court) / +1 786 621 3511
miaskateshop.com / Open daily

Because it's tucked away off the main thoroughfares, MIA Skate Shop took me a few years to find. Not that it would have meant much if I'd found it back then – at the time I didn't consider myself a skateboarder, nor did I understand its role in the local skate scene. My friend Betsy was the one who finally introduced me to this place, when she took her bike to the repair shop next door and then stopped by MIA to see an old friend. The store is small, but packs a punch thanks to the discerning eye of its owners, who've selected only the trendiest apparel and accessories. What I love most about MIA is that it doubles as a neighborhood hangout – you never know who's going to pop in to check out the new gear or to say hi.

MIAMI BEACH BOTANICAL GARDEN

Tranquil green space

2000 Convention Center Drive (near Dade Boulevard)
+1 305 673 7256 / mbgarden.org / Closed Monday

My home base may be physically located on an island next to the beach, but it's a full-blown city à la NYC. Living here brings all the stresses of urban life, combined with concrete jungle views from which I sometimes need a serious escape. The Miami Beach Botanical Garden is one such hideaway for me. It's close to my office, so I stroll over whenever I need to take a breather. The property is absolutely gorgeous – in fact, I considered holding my wedding here. My most admired areas are the Japanese Garden, for its splendor, and the natural pond, for its local plants like the red mangroves that filled the barrier island before urban development.

THE PALMS SPA

Oceanfront escape

3025 Collins Avenue (near 30th Street) / +1 305 534 0505
thepalmshotel.com / Open daily

There's just something about the Old Florida vibe: the weathered wood, the light color palettes, the low-speed fans. I love it all. The charm of The Palms Hotel is the reason I chose it to hold my Florida beach wedding, but the blissful spa is why I keep coming back. It carries the serene mood and aesthetic of a coastal cottage, and sitting in their lounge feels like relaxing in Lilly Pulitzer's Palm Beach home rather than waiting to get a treatment. My pick for relieving stress is their 80-minute rub-down, and because the spa can customize each service, I always add a warm oil infusion scalp massage, which combines to be 95 minutes of absolute, unadulterated relaxation. Bonus perks are the in-spa noshing on healthy dishes, the outdoor Tiki cabanas and full-day access to the pool.

THE WEBSTER

Luxe style

1220 Collins Avenue (near 12th Street) / +1 305 674 7899
thewebster.us / Open daily

Ever since Laure Heriard Dubreuil and Milan Vukmirovic opened their three-story, tropical-themed fashion dollhouse inside the former Webster Hotel, the stylish set has had this town on the radar. From Charlotte Olympia's palm leaf platforms to Aurélie Bidermann's Copacabana cuff in neon, Magic City references seem to be the new black. So where am I strutting my stilettos to admire that Delfina Delettrez flamingo earrings or to get my man some Orlebar Brown swim shorts? Directly to the store that put this town on the sartorial map, of course! I'm admiring all of the Miami-inspired Sophia Webster shoes in their inventory from afar (and calling dibs), but one day they shall all be mine.

YARDBIRD SOUTHERN TABLE & BAR

Southern plates with all the fixin's

1600 Lenox Avenue (at 16th Street) / +1 305 538 5220
runchickenrun.com / Open daily

This town had little to offer in terms of Southern comfort food until Yardbird brought delectable fried chicken and mama's chicken biscuits to South Beach. The country kitchen setting feels more like Georgia than Miami, but it works. In fact, the concept was so successful, it won a James Beard Award. As lip-smacking as everything is, I'm partial to the butter lettuce and grilled mango salad, and crunchy Yardbird sandwich with honey hot sauce and pickles. Beware their bourbon drinks – I've seen them (particularly the blackberry bourbon lemonade) take down many an expert imbiber with little effort.

art deco lures

Lesser known architectural attractions

11TH STREET DINER
1065 Washington Avenue (at 11th Street; Miami Beach), +1 305 534 6373
eleventhstreetdiner.com, open daily

BASS MUSEUM OF ART
2100 Collins Avenue (near 22nd Street; Miami Beach)
+1 786 436 8133, bassmuseum.org, open daily

COLONY THEATRE
1040 Lincoln Road (at Lenox Avenue; Miami Beach)
+1 305 674 1040, colonytheatremiamibeach.com
closed Sunday and Monday

MIAMI DESIGN PRESERVATION LEAGUE
1001 Ocean Drive (at 10th Street; Miami Beach)
+1 305 672 2014, mdpl.org, open daily

TOWER THEATER
1508 Southwest 8th Street (at Southwest 15th Avenue; Little Havana), +1 305 643 8706
towertheatermiami.com, open daily

BASS MUSEUM OF ART

COLONY THEATRE

Though Art Deco is not a style of architecture unique to this city, Miami Beach's Ocean Drive is one of the first places that comes to mind when someone mentions it, and for good reason. Iconic movies like *The Birdcage*, as well as franchises like *Miami Vice*, took advantage of the Art Deco Historic District's pastel-hued façades and palm tree-lined sidewalks to channel the area's tropical flair on film.

While Ocean Drive can be a tourist-laden mess, it's still worth checking out – away from the crowds – from the beachwalk that runs along the eastern side of Lummus Park. A worthy starting point is the **Miami Design Preservation League** (MDPL) building, which is the headquarters of the non-profit dedicated to preserving, protecting and promoting this style of art from the 1920s, defined by geometric motifs, curvilinear forms, sharply defined outlines and bold colors. The MDPL offers year-round programming related to the Historic District, including the annual Art Deco Weekend in January and other small events. Plus, the clock to its south and the Miami Beach Ocean Rescue Headquarters to its east are both beautiful examples of the style.

TOWER THEATER

Head one block north and two blocks west, and you'll arrive at the **11th Street Diner**, a classic Art Deco-style eatery with vinyl booths that serves comfort food with a twist. They're open late, so they're super clutch after a night on the town. If you'd rather satisfy your hunger with arts and culture, I recommend the **Colony Theatre** on Lincoln Road or the **Bass Museum of Art** in Collins Park. The former hosts live art and stage performances, while the latter specializes in exhibitions of contemporary art. Both buildings have distinctively different features, but are a sight to behold.

While the highest concentration of such architecture is in Miami Beach, there are more peppered throughout our different neighborhoods. Most have been transformed into hotels, but places like the **Tower Theater** in Little Havana have retained their individuality as a cultural landmark. The movie house, where many Cuban refugees were first introduced to American culture, is still an independent cinema regularly showing both English and Spanish language films.

downtown

midtown

Our famous skyline is a beauty to behold. One of the greatest things about the urban center is the variety of building heights and types of architecture you see. While Brickell is high-rise heavy, the heart of Downtown is home to an eclectic mix of buildings. There's '80s-heavy Bayside Marketplace, its magnanimous neighbor the AmericanAirlines Arena (Go Heat!) and the architecturally striking duo of Pérez Art Museum Miami (see pg 24) and Adrienne Arsht Center to their north. As you travel further up Biscayne Boulevard, skyscrapers give way to mid-sized buildings and eventually the single-family homes and low-rises surrounding The Shops at Midtown. This central neighborhood well encapsulates the architectural diversity for which this city is known, yes, but also in its residents and what it offers in cultural, dining and nightlife options. In fact, every time I veer off Biscayne Boulevard and get lost – which happens more often than not – I discover something new about this area.

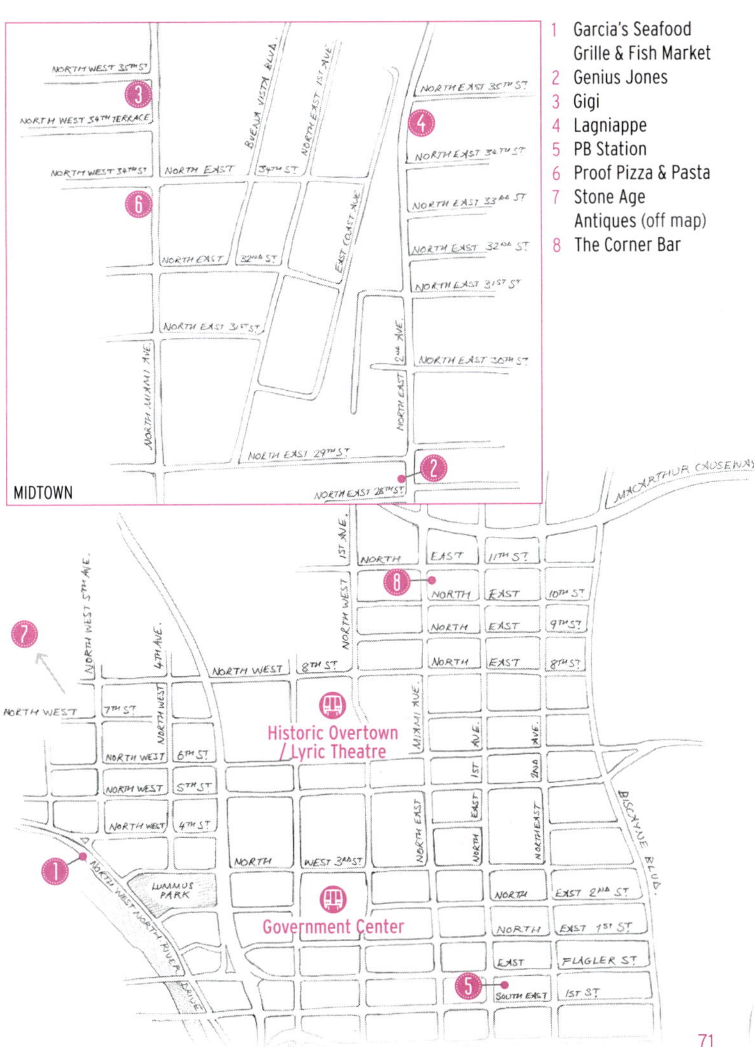
1 Garcia's Seafood Grille & Fish Market
2 Genius Jones
3 Gigi
4 Lagniappe
5 PB Station
6 Proof Pizza & Pasta
7 Stone Age Antiques (off map)
8 The Corner Bar
MIDTOWN
Historic Overtown / Lyric Theatre
Government Center
NORTH WEST 35TH ST
NORTH WEST 34TH TERRACE
NORTH WEST 34TH ST
NORTH EAST 34TH ST
BUENA VISTA BLVD.
NORTH EAST 1ST AVE.
NORTH EAST 35TH ST
NORTH EAST 33RD ST
NORTH EAST 32ND ST
NORTH EAST 31ST ST
NORTH EAST 30TH ST
NORTH EAST 29TH ST
NORTH EAST 28TH ST
EAST COAST AVE.
NORTH EAST 2ND AVE.
NORTH MIAMI AVE.
MACARTHUR CAUSEWAY
NORTH WEST 1ST AVE.
NORTH EAST 11TH ST
NORTH EAST 10TH ST
NORTH EAST 9TH ST
NORTH EAST 8TH ST
NORTH WEST 8TH ST
NORTH WEST 5TH AVE.
NORTH WEST 4TH AVE.
NORTH WEST 7TH ST
NORTH WEST 6TH ST
NORTH WEST 5TH ST
NORTH WEST 4TH ST
NORTH WEST 3RD ST
MIAMI AVE.
NORTH EAST 1ST AVE.
NORTH EAST 2ND AVE.
BISCAYNE BLVD.
NORTH EAST 2ND ST
NORTH EAST 1ST ST
EAST FLAGLER ST
SOUTH EAST 1ST ST
LUMMUS PARK
NORTH WEST NORTH RIVER DRIVE

GARCIA'S SEAFOOD GRILLE & FISH MARKET

Casual riverfront eats

398 Northwest North River Drive (at Northwest 4th Street)
+1 305 375 0765 / garciasmiami.com / Open daily

Garcia's is a time capsule. Yes, it's waterfront dining but, unlike the bougie hot spots that have recently popped up along the Miami River, it retains the rustic charm of the area's humble origins when rugged fishermen – some of whom are still around – hung out on their houseboats grilling their catch of the day and downing bourbon. This nostalgic appeal and long-standing relationship with the city makes Garcia's an affordable spot that draws the who's who of Miami, all under the premise of deliciously straightforward seafood dishes. (The complimentary fish dip and their grilled fish sandwiches are must-haves.) Their outdoor dock is one of my favorite lunch spots and where I always take out-of-town guests.

GENIUS JONES

High-quality goodies for children

2800 Northeast 2nd Avenue (at Northeast 28th Street)
+1 305 571 2000 / geniusjones.com / Open daily

In a time when specialty boutiques were being forced to close their doors, Daniel Kron found himself in need of a bigger space to fill with miniature Panton chairs and neon-colored strollers, so he moved into the Miami Design District. His winning concept? The notion that you're entering parenthood doesn't mean you have to surrender your home's elegant aesthetic to a jumble of playthings. At his store, which recently relocated to Midtown, you will find well-crafted, design-inspired alternatives that are both functional and aesthetically pleasing when compared to the plastic toys of today. The shop's collection is what you'd expect to see if the head of the MoMA was asked to curate children's items – which is likely why the art-obsessed are fans.

GIGI

Asian comfort food and noodle bar

3470 North Miami Avenue (at Northwest 35th Street)
+1 305 573 1520 / giginow.com / Open daily

In the months following Gigi's 2010 debut, it was all anyone could talk about but it was out of pure rebellion that I delayed my first visit. One Saturday at 2am, my friends and I left a concert absolutely starving and I finally caved because Gigi was close by and open. Despite the late hour, the place was packed. We scored seats at the bar and were entertained by the action in the open kitchen. Of the several dishes we tried, we found none we did not love, from their burger to their 8 oz filet in sriracha butter to their chilled soba noodles and everything in between. My only grouse? Not allowing myself to discover Gigi's greatness sooner.

LAGNIAPPE

New Orleans-style wine bar

3425 Northeast 2nd Avenue (near Northeast 35th Street)
+1 305 576 0108 / lagniappehouse.com / Open daily

One of the problems with living in a densely urbanized environment is the limited access to outdoor space, which, considering the city's amazing climate, is an absolute sin. Enter Lagniappe, a watering hole that has a lovely yard outfitted with mismatched chairs and mesmerizing string lights. Although it's nestled in the busy Midtown area, this secluded spot's landscaping and nightly live music give off a calming suburban mood instead of a typical city feel. In fact, it's the closest I've gotten to recreating the magical nights of watching the stars in a friend's backyard since my university days. The staff are knowledgeable and helpful, and are an excellent resource for food and vino pairings. I usually go for the charcuterie board and barbecued churrasco platter with a bottle of red. So much yes.

PB STATION

Mod American fare

121 Southeast 1st Street (near Northeast 1st Avenue)
+1 305 420 2205 / pbstation.com / Open daily

Located on the ground floor of the Langford Hotel, within a stunning space previously occupied by a bank, PB Station is a winning concept from restaurateur geniuses, the Pubbelly Boys. I love the location because it's a nod to the days when Downtown was the city's business hub (a role that Brickell has commandeered in recent years). The menu is on point, delivering chef Jose Mendin's characteristic take on international eats through the lens of New American cuisine in dishes like French onion soup dumplings and yellowtail ceviche tacos. If you're in the area and don't have time to linger over dinner, I recommend at least stopping by the bar. Try the Booze Hound – a twist on the Mexican Paloma – or the Damned and Beautiful – a concoction of Champagne, St. George vodka, blackberry gastrique and pink peppercorn and sugar rim. You'll thank me later!

PROOF PIZZA & PASTA

Delish Italian eats

3328 North Miami Avenue (at Northwest 34th Street)
+1 786 536 9562 / proofpizza.com / Closed Monday

My first visit here was unforgettable. My friend Jamison and I had an absolutely delightful evening dining outdoors in their super cute terrace with its rows of twinkling lights. But it was not just the ambiance that I loved. I still daydream about the gemelli bolognese in all its fresh basil and whipped ricotta goodness, and how good it tasted accompanied by a glass of Cabernet and finished with a macaron ice cream sandwich. My mouth is watering just thinking about the meal. But until my next visit, I'll have to make do with salivating over Instagram pictures of their food.

STONE AGE ANTIQUES

Maritime antiques off the beaten path

3236 Northwest South River Drive (near Northwest 32nd Avenue)
+1 305 633 5114 / stoneage-antiques.com / Closed Saturday and Sunday

As a marine science geek, the archive that Milton Stone has amassed at Stone Age Antiques is an absolute delight that draws out a childlike giddiness in me and may have made me forget the "don't touch" rule once or twice. I'm not alone in my admiration of his eclectic inventory: this place is a go-to not just for those in the market for nautical décor, but also for movie crews looking for props like wooden mermaid busts and old shipwreck artifacts. In fact, he started the business following his role as a prop stylist for the TV show *Flipper* in the '60s. Stone can seem a little formidable, but I get the feeling that he is a fan of visitors, particularly ones who can appreciate his special collection of old ship windows, oversized knots et al. If you like the ocean, this is most certainly the place for you.

THE CORNER

Live jazz, small bites and handcrafted cocktails

1035 North Miami Avenue (at Northwest 11th Street)
+1 305 961 7887 / thecornermiami.com / Open daily

The intersection of 11th Street and North Miami Avenue is, for me, one of the most intimidating corners in Downtown because it is low-lit and in a rough area. That said, I still make the occasional trek there because it is home to one of the city's key watering holes: The Corner. The interior is reminiscent of a Prohibition-Era joint, and while it is marvelous on weekends, I prefer to visit during the weekday happy hour (between 4pm and 8pm) for well-priced drinks accompanied by grub from their snack menu (don't skip the empanadas or spicy chips). My husband loves their craft beer flights, and I opt for the Hot and Smoky (mezcal, lime, cane sugar and dried habanero) or La Tacubaya (tequila, Green Chartreuse, lime, hibiscus, agave and habanero bitters). I also religiously check their Facebook page for the weekly live jazz lineup.

MIAMI AFTER DARK: mad about mojitos

Awesome takes on the Cuban cocktail

LARIOS ON THE BEACH

Despite Miami's proximity to Cuba, the mojito didn't reach our shores until after it had made its way across Europe and into remote parts of Britain. Nevertheless, this city is now a second home to the drink, due to our close ties to Cuban culture. While the mojito's birthplace and even its name have been a topic of discussion amongst historians, I really don't care where it comes from or what it's called so long as it tastes good. Personally, I think the Cubans said "to hell with plain old boring lemonade" and created their own indisputably ingenious, boozy solution to a hot summer's day.

My most-loved recipe to date is the classic take, which is made from locally sourced ingredients typical to the island, including white rum, gently crushed mint leaves, lime and raw cane sugar or guarapo (sugarcane juice). You'll find it, along with a bajillion variations in just about every restaurant or bar. For a taste of how it's done in Cuba, **Larios on the Beach** (owned by Gloria and Emilio Estefan) is where to go. Similarly, Coral Gables' choice Caribbean spot, **Ortanique on the Mile**, is another recommended venue for the bona fide concoction.

Looking for a twist inspired by the city's melting pot of cultures? Refined eatery **Casa Tua** allows you to pair the sweet drink with the bright flavors of the Mediterranean. Not to be outdone, downtown Peruvian staple **CVI.CHE 105** has taken the liberty of adding a pisco flourish. If you think that's bold, **Sugarcane Raw Bar Grill** in Midtown, the neighborhood famous for blending foods of all cultures, has created the beet mojito – a delish libation that is bound to leave you wondering what other tasty sips you can make with vegetables and alcohol.

Whether you go traditional or not, drinking a mojito is one of those must-do things to cross off your list while you're here. So, why not do it where they serve the finest?

CASA TUA
1700 James Avenue (at 17th Street; Miami Beach)
+1 305 673 1010, casatualifestyle.com/miami, open daily

CVI.CHE 105
105 Northeast 3rd Avenue (near Northeast 1st Street; Downtown), +1 305 577 3454
ceviche105.com/downtownmiami, open daily

LARIOS ON THE BEACH
820 Ocean Drive (near 8th Street; Miami Beach)
+1 305 532 9577, lariosonthebeach.com, open daily

ORTANIQUE ON THE MILE
278 Miracle Mile (near Salzedo Street; Coral Gables)
+1 305 446 7710, ortaniquerestaurants.com
open daily

SUGARCANE RAW BAR GRILL
3252 Northeast 1st Avenue (at Northeast 32nd Street; Midtown), +1 786 369 0353, sugarcanerawbargrill.com
open daily

MIAMI AFTER DARK: city soundtrack

Groove to the beat

In the age of electronic music and highly produced beats, it's super easy to find when and where a DJ is playing in one of the many nightclubs. But finding a live music hangout can seem to be a bit of a chore, which is a shame considering Miami's cultural roots stem from much deeper and rugged humble musical beginnings. Legends like Nat King Cole, Aretha Franklin and Celia Cruz once took center stage here, and it's their influences that continue to be the undertones to the music I still associate with my city. I'm happy to report that if you want to escape the *untz-untz-untz* of nightlife, this city's live music venues have a lot to offer. You just have to know where to look.

THE ELECTRIC PICKLE COMPANY

Music runs so deep in our veins that you can actually find its presence in just about any neighborhood, with Little Havana at the epicenter of the Latin set. Along the historical street of Calle Ocho, places like Hoy Como Ayer (see pg 92) and **Cubaocho Museum & Performing Arts Center** – a bar, gallery and performing arts venue rolled into one – are some of the choice spots to experience Cuban music at its least adulterated.

Less than a 10-minute drive east toward Brickell, **El Tucán** delivers a swankier cabaret rendition of the same. The best part? These two venues are enjoyable at any age, so whether you're in town with your friends or visiting your grandparents, they can add some spice to your itinerary.

Beyond Latin music, this town has a few spots that nod to its past, like **The Regent Cocktail Club**, a speakeasy-style lounge situated in a space previously occupied by The Regent, a hotel that opened in 1941. This Art Deco-inspired live music venue takes guests back to the '40s with its traditional jazz and drinks menu, which centers around classic cocktails like the Old Fashioned.

Building on the momentum of our musical foundation, a newer generation of homegrown artists is defining the local sound with regular performances throughout the city. **Bougainvillea's Old Florida Tavern**, or "Bougies" is ideal for anyone able to kick back and groove to any music genre. Tuesday through Sunday, local acts electrify the tavern and its outdoor patio with everything from jazz and R&B to reggae and rock.

Similarly, **Bardot** and **The Electric Pickle Company** regularly hold killer performances by underground talents of all genres. In fact, one of the top five concerts I've seen was when my friend MJ's band, Awesome New Republic, played to an intimate crowd at the former a few years back.

BARDOT
3456 North Miami Avenue (near Northwest 35th Street; Midtown), +1 305 576 5570
bardotmiami.com, closed Sunday and Monday

BOUGAINVILLEA'S OLD FLORIDA TAVERN
7221 Southwest 58th Avenue (near Southwest 73rd Street; South Miami), +1 305 669 8577
bougiesbar.com, open daily

CUBAOCHO MUSEUM & PERFORMING ARTS CENTER
1465 Southwest 8th Street Suite 106 (at Southwest 15th Avenue; Little Havana), +1 305 285 5880
cubaocho.com, closed Sunday

EL TUCÁN
1111 Southwest 1st Avenue (near Southwest 11th Street; Downtown), +1 305 535 0065
eltucanmiami.com, open Thursday through Saturday

THE ELECTRIC PICKLE COMPANY
2826 North Miami Avenue (near Northwest 29th Street; Wynwood), +1 305 456 5613
electricpicklemiami.com
open Wednesday through Saturday

THE REGENT COCKTAIL CLUB
1690 Collins Avenue (near 17th Street; Miami Beach), +1 786 975 2555, regentcocktailclub.com, open daily

EL TUCÁN

little havana

west miami

When I'm looking for the ultimate Miami experience, I head to Little Havana. The neighborhood's pivotal role as a second home to exiled Cubans is memorialized by cafés, fruit stands, cigar shops, rooster sculptures and landmarks such as Domino Park. But this enclave – which, for the record, extends far beyond Calle Ocho – has also become a popular refuge for Nicaraguans, Hondurans, Mexicans and other immigrants, and their influence is undeniable: the Cuban Walk of Fame has become the Latin Walk of Fame, and the Annual Calle Ocho Festival has become as much about celebrating Cuban heritage as it is about celebrating the culture of Central and South American countries. There's a lot to explore, including the gorgeous bungalow-style homes peppered throughout the residential zones, so I recommend getting an introduction to the area at the free walking tour during Viernes Culturales (the last Friday of every month) or signing up for the Miami Culinary Tour for an overview of this expansive neighborhood.

WEST FLAGLER ST
NORTH WEST 57TH AVE.
SOUTH WEST 8TH ST
SOUTH WEST 16TH ST
CORAL WAY
3
6
WEST MIAMI

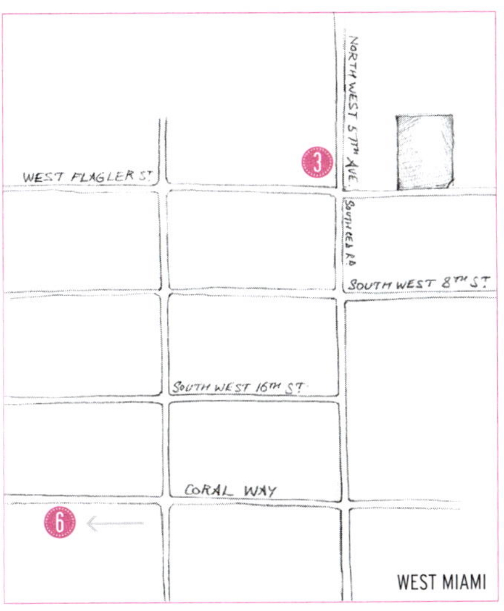

1 Azucar Ice Cream Company
2 Ball & Chain
3 El Palacio de los Jugos
4 El Rey de las Fritas
5 Hoy Como Ayer
6 Islas Canarias Restaurant (off map)
7 Jamon Iberico Pata Negra Restaurant (off map)
8 La Camaronera
9 Little Havana Cigar Factory

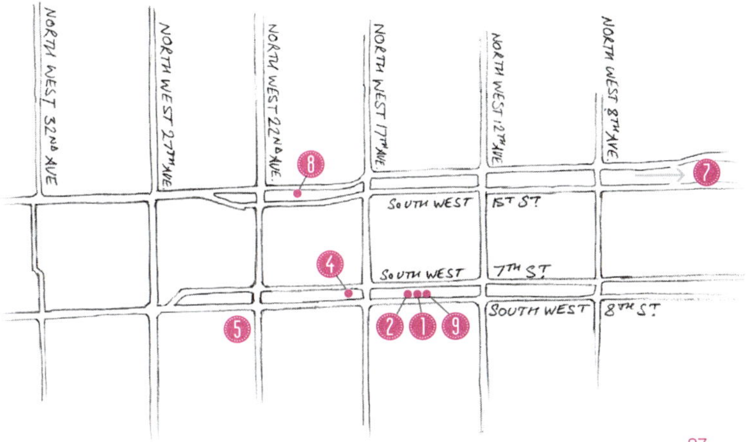

NORTH WEST 32ND AVE
NORTH WEST 27TH AVE
NORTH WEST 22ND AVE.
NORTH WEST 17TH AVE.
NORTH WEST 12TH AVE.
NORTH WEST 8TH AVE.
SOUTH WEST 1ST ST
SOUTH WEST 7TH ST
SOUTH WEST 8TH ST
8
7
4
5
2
1
9

AZUCAR ICE CREAM COMPANY

Gourmet frozen sweets

1503 Southwest 8th Street (at Southwest 15th Avenue)
+1 305 381 0369 / azucaricecream.com / Open daily

If you ever want to elicit a childlike squeal from any Latino, bring up *galletas Maria*. Whether it was our mom or our grandmom or our aunt who proffered them, these cookies were a staple of our childhoods. My mom gave them to me for everything, as a lunch treat smeared in Mexican cajeta (caramel) and as a stomach remedy served plain. (Don't ask – I never did.) Susan Batlle's homemade ice cream flavors play on that nostalgia to bring unexpected and utterly local flavors like café con leche, mamey and flan. The Abuela Maria is her signature and most popular treat. She spent a long time working with friends to perfect a recipe that transforms vanilla ice cream with large chunks of galletas Maria, guava paste and cream cheese into absolute ambrosial magic.

BALL & CHAIN

Historic watering hole with live music

1513 Southwest 8th Street (near Southwest 15th Street)
+1 305 643 7820 / ballandchainmiami.com / Open daily

One of Little Havana's icons is this hot spot, which opened on Calle Ocho in 1935. In the 1950s, it played host to top-tier entertainers including Count Basie and Billie Holiday. It closed for several years following its heyday until it was renovated and reopened in 2014. The venue has now restored its role in the city's music scene, hosting local acts from Thursday through Sunday. It gets busier the later you go, so if you don't like crowds or are looking for dancing room, I recommend arriving earlier. My preferred time to stop by is during happy hour (4pm to 7pm) when I can sit back and relax in their outdoor patio, a *pastelito* daiquiri in hand.

EL PALACIO DE LOS JUGOS

Hispanic street food

5721 West Flagler Street (at Northwest 57th Avenue)
+1 305 264 8662 / elpalaciodelosjugos.com / Open daily

So you did the fancy hotel restaurant thing, emptied your wallet, but still feel hungry. Don't worry, I've been there and done that. It's almost a rite of passage and is easily cured by heading to El Palacio de los Jugos for a hearty, easy and no-frills meal. Here you'll fill up with Cuban nosh, such as the maduro frita (fried sweet plantains), pan con lechón (roast pork sandwiches) and coco frio (fresh coconut juice) for less than last night's valet tip. Granted, the low-key ambiance is miles away from the Fontainebleau's glitz and glamour, but there's a certain charm to this colorful outdoor food market with patrons slurping up juice and chowing down on fried pork cracklings.

EL REY DE LAS FRITAS

Home of the Cuban burger

1821 Southwest 8th Street (near Southwest 18th Avenue)
+1 305 644 6054 / elreydelasfritas.com / Open daily

El Rey de las Fritas literally means "The King of Burgers," which is ironic given that a certain major fast food chain with a similar name is headquartered here. But, a frita Cubana, or Cuban hamburger, isn't run-of-the-mill. On the contrary, a frita is an ultra-juicy patty loaded with secret sauce and spices, chopped onions and Pik-Nik chips between a sweet, fluffy bun. Like Philly has its cheesesteak rivalries, we have our frita contentions, but there can only be one king. So grab a seat at the counter and ask for a batido de mamey (Caribbean fruit smoothie) to go with your frita. You're in good hands.

HOY COMO AYER

Atmospheric bar and lounge with music

2212 Southwest 8th Street
(near Southwest 22nd Avenue)
+1 305 541 2631 / hoycomoayer.us
Open Thursday through Sunday

Hoy Como Ayer is where you should be if your idea of going out involves dancing like nobody's watching. The mainstay is popular for its live Cuban music, drinks and salsa dancing. My friend Corinna, who lives and breathes Little Havana, is always raving about the intoxicating energy of this intimate venue. Check the programming calendar on their website and, if your schedule allows, take the opportunity to see artists like Spam Allstars, who usually perform on Thursday nights. Note that the website is only in Spanish, so you may need a translator to navigate your way around. Also, this venue runs on Miami time (that is, late), so don't expect to see the main act until around midnight.

ISLAS CANARIAS RESTAURANT

Scrumptious croquetas

13695 Southwest 26th Street (at Coral Way) / +1 305 559 6666
islascanariasrestaurant.com / Open daily

The tastiest things are worth driving for, and they definitely include the famous croquetas at Islas Canarias. When I have visitors, the number one responsibility I feel as a Miamian is to introduce them to this place. The version here is made from a secret recipe that has been passed down generations. If given the chance, I would drown myself in their deep-fried, breaded nuggets of ham and goodness. Beyond these fried bites, Islas offers the full Cuban dining experience, including a basket of buttery toast to start, sides of white rice and beans with your main course and a server in a curve-accentuating polyester uniform calling you "mama" as she refills your water.

JAMON IBERICO PATA NEGRA RESTAURANT

Welcoming Spanish dining spot

10 Southwest South River Drive (near West Flagler Street)
+1 305 324 1111 / patanegrarestaurant.com / Open daily

Food service in this town is well-known for leaning toward impersonal and absent-minded. Perhaps it's the transient nature of most customers, or the blend of different cultures that wears down our industry staff. Nevertheless, we appreciate excellent treatment when we get it and in no place is it more obvious than at Jamon Iberico Pata Negra Restaurant. Chef Felipe Pérez greets you with the excitement of a father welcoming his prodigal child back home. Throughout a delectable meal of conventional eats, including tapas such as Galician-style octopus and a lip-smacking serrano ham and Manchego combo, he will chat and thank you for letting him feed you. I've yet to meet a more passionate business owner, and for all these reasons (plus the incredible food), this is a place you just cannot miss.

LA CAMARONERA

Seafood counter experience

1952 West Flagler Street (near Southwest 20th Avenue)
+1 305 642 3322 / garciabrothersseafood.com / Open daily

This Little Havana locale started off as a fish market when the Garcia brothers came here from Cuba, escaping Fidel Castro's communist regime in the 1960s. A decade later, they found that some patrons wanted to enjoy the catch of the day right then and there, so they added kitchen equipment and started serving up their now-famous deep-fried shrimp and fish sandwiches. Today, not much has changed: the counters still get packed during lunch at "los paraditos" or "the standing ones" (the nickname given by old-school patrons referring to lack of stools) and service is speedy, so don't get too comfortable. The market still remains, which means you can buy fresh ceviche or an entire grouper to make your own pan con minuta (fried fish sandwich) at home if you aren't eating there.

LITTLE HAVANA CIGAR FACTORY

Family-owned cigar emporium

1501 Southwest 8th Street (at Southwest 15th Avenue)
+1 305 541 1035 / lhcfstore.com / Open daily

There's something to be said about roaming around this shop, inhaling the nuanced aromas, taking your pick, then savoring it slowly. While smoking is not for me, I appreciate a good old-fashioned tobacco experience. I first tried it on a night out on the town with my husband and friends. We started at Ball & Chain (see pg 89) and decided to stop here for a puff on my friend Nate's recommendation. Nate knows cigars, so his confidence in their inventory has made this my pit stop when I'm looking for a gift.

local flavor

Homegrown eats

MIAMI SMOKERS

One of the most frequent requests I get from readers of my blog is for dishes they can eat only here. When I first started fielding these requests, my default response was to send them to the closest place with a decent Cuban sandwich and colada (Cuban espresso), and that was that. But, after a while, I realized they weren't asking for my expertise in identifying the items they already knew they had to try. Rather, they needed my help in finding these less-obvious meals that exhibit Miami's coveted Latin flair. Because I pride myself in being a valuable resource, I revised my list accordingly.

Worthy venues are spots like **Miami Smokers**, an urban smokehouse and deli in Little Havana that serves pork-heavy variations on Cuban standards including bacon-wrapped plantains, an El Cubano sandwich and a Havana Club sandwich that includes lechón (suckling pig) and avocado, with the usual suspects. Likewise, **Sakaya Kitchen** in Midtown serves up an Asian twist to the popular croquetas by filling them with housemade dae ji (marinated spicy pork) instead of the conventional ham. Also on my list is

MY CEVICHE

Eating House Miami in Coral Gables, where chef Giorgio Rapicavoli combines local ingredients for one-of-a-kind items like the Calentado wrap of pork, maduros (fried plantains) and congri (black beans and rice). Across the bridge in the Beach, **My Ceviche** blends ceviche-based bites with Mexican touches in menu offerings like rare tuna tacos with tomatillo salsa and octopus burritos with spicy jalapeño mayo. Don't be fooled by their miniscule venue – after all, big things come in small packages.

If you're more of a traditionalist, ultra-relaxed and less-hipster joint **Yambo Restaurant** reminds us that our cuisine is not only about Cuban food, with homestyle Nicaraguan fare like carne asada (grilled beef) platters and queso frito (fried cheese) that are absolutely delish. Similarly, **Jimmy'z Kitchen** in Wynwood has won over the hearts of Puerto Ricans and non-Puerto Ricans alike with one of the top mofongos (mashed fried plantains) in town despite looking like your run-of-the-mill café. So, take my recommendations and savor these before you leave my city.

EATING HOUSE MIAMI
804 Ponce De Leon Boulevard (near Southwest 8th Street; Coral Gables), +1 305 448 6524
eatinghousemiami.com, open daily

JIMMY'Z KITCHEN
2700 North Miami Avenue (near Northeast 27th Street; Wynwood), +1 305 573 1505
jimmyzkitchen.com, open daily

MIAMI SMOKERS
306 Northwest 27th Avenue (at Northwest 3rd Street; Little Havana), +1 786 520 5420, miamismokers.com
closed Sunday

MY CEVICHE
235 Washington Avenue (near 3rd Street; Miami Beach), +1 305 397 8710, myceviche.com
open daily

SAKAYA KITCHEN
3401 North Miami Avenue #125 (near Northeast 36th Street; Midtown), +1 305 576 8096
sakayakitchen.com, open daily

YAMBO RESTAURANT
1643 Southwest 1st Street (near Southwest 17th Avenue; Little Havana), +1 305 649 0203
facebook.com/YamboRestaurant, open daily

coral gables and south miami

When I chose to study at the University of Miami, I knew absolutely nothing about Coral Gables or South Miami. My only exposure was during a high school summer program, where my off-campus exploits involved the T.G.I. Friday's and the CVS pharmacy across the street. But four years here revealed two vibrant, primarily residential communities that are so much more than the chain stores along US1. The main drag of downtown Coral Gables, called Miracle Mile, boasts captivating storefronts housing restaurants, salons and boutiques. As for South Miami, the commercial district conveys a main street charm with its small shops and rows of sidewalk cafés along Sunset Drive. It's these attributes that captivated my dad and convinced him this was the right place for his daughter to leave home at the age of 18. While Miami Beach is much more fitting for this stage in my life, I make regular weekend visits to both Coral Gables and South Miami – my best friend Morgan in tow – to reminisce about my first years of independence in this city.

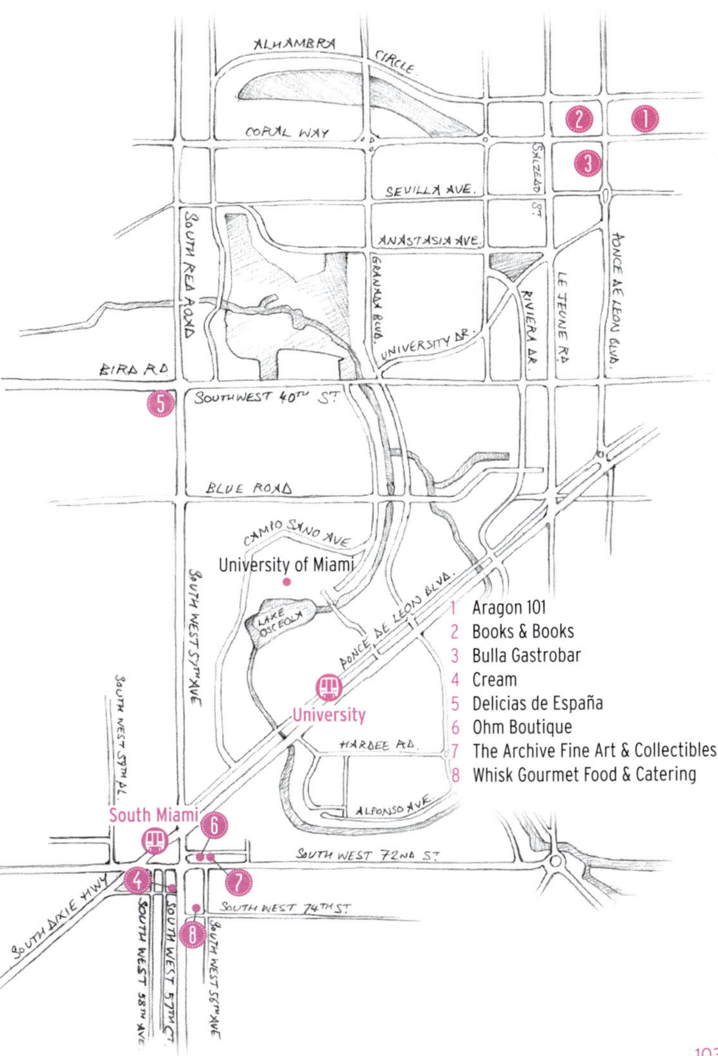

1 Aragon 101
2 Books & Books
3 Bulla Gastrobar
4 Cream
5 Delicias de España
6 Ohm Boutique
7 The Archive Fine Art & Collectibles
8 Whisk Gourmet Food & Catering

ARAGON 101

Home décor and cooking school

101 Aragon Avenue (near Galiano Street) / +1 305 443 7335
aragon101.com / Closed Sunday

At Aragon 101, Erica Guzman demonstrates how a fantastic meal is instantly elevated by the right ambiance. Here, you can pick up culinary skills – she holds in-store cooking classes about once a week that are a mix of interactive and demonstrative, focused on teaching you approachable recipes (everything from homemade tiramisu and limoncello to dim sum and tagines) that you can (and will) repeat at home. You can also conveniently shop for kitchen goodies and tableware to match your newly acquired chops and throw a proper dinner party. If you'd rather someone else do the cooking, keep a lookout for the supper club schedules on the website.

BOOKS & BOOKS

RECOMMENDED BY
ANNIE VAZQUEZ
FOUNDER OF THEFASHIONPOET.COM

Well-loved literary hangout

265 Aragon Avenue (near Salzedo Street) / +1 305 442 4408
booksandbooks.com/coralgables / Open daily

Mitchell Kaplan hit it out of the park when he founded Books & Books. This welcoming Coral Gables outpost is the original, and boasts a wide selection of titles. It's one of my preferred places to cuddle up with a good book – I usually pick one of the staff's recommendations – and a cup of coffee or glass of prosecco in hand. With its wooden floors and rows of bookcases, the interior reminds me of when I used to spend the day in the library as a kid, getting lost in story after story. The Mediterranean-style building it calls home surrounds an open-air courtyard that's lovely for a long, leisurely lunch with my girlfriends. To round out the Books & Books experience, Kaplan regularly lures literary notables for author events, so be sure to check and see who might be doing a talk and signing their new release when you're in town.

BULLA GASTROBAR

Spanish decadence

2500 Ponce De Leon Boulevard (at Andalusia Avenue)
+1 305 441 0107 / bullagastrobar.com / Open daily

I passed by Bulla at least a thousand times without setting foot inside – despite always being packed, it just never really drew my attention. In fact, my first visit was at the request of my friend Lou, a Miami native who was moving to San Diego and planned his goodbye dinner there. "Bulla?" I asked. "Bulla!" he replied. With this one excited syllable, Lou vastly improved my life because that night I was introduced to huevos Bulla, one of my most-loved dishes. It's an unapologetically decadent combination of homemade potato chips topped with a jumbo poached egg, serrano ham, potato foam and a generous drizzle of truffle oil. Yes, the menu has less indulgent fare but when you go, you absolutely cannot miss this.

CREAM

A beauty aficionado's heaven

5731 Southwest 73rd Street (near Southwest 57th Avenue)
+1 305 669 9220 / creambeauty.com / Closed Sunday

I don't usually wear makeup, but I have an unhealthy obsession with skincare lines that give me a natural glow. I browse rows of lipsticks and eye shadows with little interest, but if you swing me by a counter of moisturizers and serums, I might as well sign over my paycheck to the employee at the register. In Cream, Tamra Gordon has put together my ideal treasure chest by stocking brands like Rodin Oil, Mario Badescu and Korres alongside Bond No. 9 candles and Creed perfume. This shop is also a salon, where you can get a make-over with products by respected cosmetic brands like NARS, a mani-pedi and even have your brows shaped.

DELICIAS DE ESPAÑA

Flamenco in your mouth

4016 Southwest 57th Avenue (at Southwest 40th Street)
+1 305 669 4485 / deliciasdeespana.com / Open daily

Delicias de España started as a two-table restaurant in a corner shopping center and, in a decade, has grown into a three-venue institution. The Coral Gables location, where Ernesto Llerandi and his wife first set up shop, has expanded to include a much larger dining area and a food market selling some fantastic cocktail hour bites such as cheeses, cured meats and olives imported from Spain. The most recent addition is a boutique where you can pick up gifts like housewares and fashion from Seville. I have to thank my dad for introducing me to this place and for indirectly raising my cholesterol levels with all the boards of *jamón y queso* I've eaten here since.

OHM BOUTIQUE

Clutch women's clothing

1561 Sunset Drive (near Southwest 57th Avenue) / +1 305 284 8455
ohmboutique.com / Open daily

Someone recently asked me how I define my personal style, and when I couldn't find the right words, I told them to look at Ohm Boutique's inventory. The items in my closet that get the most wear are a gray chunky knit tank and a pair of high-waisted, wide-leg pants that came from their store. Not surprisingly, these are the clothes that make me feel like a million bucks (maybe because they get me the most compliments). If you're looking for fab quality ensembles in neutrals, this is the place. Oh, and if you're the Ohm Boutique buyer and you're reading this, I beg you to come stock my closet with the on-point and comfy pieces you've found for them. Please and thank you.

THE ARCHIVE FINE ART & COLLECTIBLES

Destination boutique with one-of-a-kind décor

1559 1/2 Sunset Drive (near Southwest 56th Avenue)
+1 305 662 4040 / thearchive-gallery.com / Closed Monday

The cost of living here means most residents, including me, rent instead of own. Although I've lived in my current beachside apartment for over four years, I've had a hard time making it feel like home. Finding the right furnishings is a key component in this endeavor; luckily, Ana Mari and Alicia have built an incredible little gallery of curated goods. From vintage tins to restored furniture, their inventory is full of inspiring finds. My biggest draw to their boutique is the paintings from South Florida artists, because nothing gives me more joy than supporting local talent.

WHISK GOURMET FOOD & CATERING

Comfort eats

7382 Southwest 56th Avenue (near Southwest 74th Street)
+1 786 268 8350 / whiskgourmet.com / Open daily

As my friends have begun having kids, they're also buying homes and settling down in quieter neighborhoods such as Coral Gables and South Miami. Knowing there are restaurants like Whisk that push the culinary envelope and create a fun atmosphere make it all the more exciting to visit said friends. Okay, so it's not really that much of a chore to visit my pal Carlos's new house for a barbecue by his pool, but it's a much more appealing proposition when I know the trip will also involve a rendezvous here for the lip-smacking fried green tomato sandwich, blue crab and roasted corn fried rice. It's all about incentive, baby.

dress the part

Look like a local

Due to the city's wonderful climate and international influences, the Miami look has come to be defined by a relaxed elegance based on light, airy fabrics in white or vibrant colors, complete with beachy accessories. I'm talking about billowy maxi dresses with sun hats, sunnies and sandals. In this city, we have learned to put these items together such that they complement us without looking like we're trying too hard – or, God forbid, like we're extras in *Scarface*. Looking good empowers me, so I'm always on the prowl for the "So Miami" get-up. Luckily, there are many top-notch boutiques nearby that cater to this chic aesthetic.

No design embodies that signature look like the boldly colored boho clothing sold at **Ramona La Rue by Arianne**. The dreamy creations by the Coconut Grove native – particularly her dresses and jumpsuits – always make me feel amazing. The threads at **Roses and Dreams** in South Beach also provide the comfort and "wow" factor with sophisticated, Parisian-inspired cuts and fabrics. The other draw for me is that owner Valérie Engel, who is super charismatic and has worked at Chanel, is available to dish out style advice like a surrogate bestie.

Speaking of BFFs, **My Best Friend's Closet** in Coral Gables is just the ticket if you're looking to blend aspects of the Miami look into a less-compatible personal style. As its name implies, the store is stocked to the brim with everything you want or could want to borrow (ahem, steal) from your girlfriend's closet, including one-of-a-kind accessories like dainty pieces by Melanie Auld and sunnies by House of Harlow.

For high-quality basics that I can dress up or down to balance bright colors and busy patterns, I rely on **Frankie** in Sunset Harbour and **MVM Miami** in Wynwood, which have racks upon racks of minimalistic yet breathtaking pieces that just speak to me. I love to pair them with **Tupelo Honey**'s covetable denim for an effortless look. I also swing by here to check out the men's section: think soft, light sweatshirts, T-shirts and trendy button downs. Whether I'm dressing for a beach day, a night out or a leisurely day about town, there is nothing that can get in my way when my get-up is flawless.

FRANKIE
1891 Purdy Avenue (near 18th Street; Miami Beach)
+1 786 479 4898, frankiemiami.com, open daily

MY BEST FRIEND'S CLOSET BOUTIQUE
68 Miracle Mile (near Galiano Street; Coral Gables)
+1 305 443 4840, mybestfriendscloset.com
open daily

MVM MIAMI
175 Northwest 23rd Street (at Northwest 2nd Avenue; Wynwood), +1 305 573 4885, mvmmiami.com
closed Sunday

RAMONA LA RUE BY ARIANNE
3400 North Miami Avenue (at Northeast 34th Street; Midtown), +1 305 456 8191, ramonalarue.com
open daily

ROSES AND DREAMS
40 South Pointe Drive #103 (near Ocean Drive; Miami Beach), +1 786 803 8383, rosesanddreams.us
open daily

TUPELO HONEY
7250 Southwest 57th Avenue (at Southwest 73rd Street; South Miami), +1 305 667 2400
tupelohoneyshop.com, open daily

coconut grove

Coconut Grove is the enclave that best personifies the relaxed Old Miami feel. Coincidentally, "the Grove" is the oldest continuously inhabited neighborhood in this city, and manages to reinvent itself time and again in spite of recent challenges like over-commercialization and economic downturn. The limestone walls, well-preserved landmarks and lush, mature trees are a constant reminder, amidst the change, of its deep-rooted history. Even more so, these elements make it one of my choice areas to visit on the weekends or when I need a break from fast-paced urban life. It is absolute bliss to drive, windows down, on Old Cutler Road with a belly full of brunch, listening to Jack Johnson and taking in the fresh, salty, subtropical scent. If the weather's pleasant and I'm looking to extend my stay, I'll end the day with a leisurely stroll or bike ride through the Grove's waterfront parks.

1 Golden Bar
2 Jaguar
3 Le Bouchon Du Grove
4 LoKal
5 The Barnacle Historic State Park
6 The Bookstore in the Grove
7 The Kampong

GOLDEN BAR

Well-curated lifestyle boutique

3092 Fuller Street (near Main Highway) / +1 305 444 4474
golden.bar / Open daily

Golden Bar is the kind of shop where, after a couple of minutes inside, you silently count the days until your birthday, Valentine's Day and Christmas because their entire inventory immediately makes it onto your wish list. Whether it's the glass vessel dangling a beta fish from the ceiling, the Turkish hammam towels, Moroccan salad servers or an antiquated typewriter sitting on the table, everything grabs your attention. Against the back wall, rustic wire shelves display a variety of games and toys that were played well before smartphones existed. Mementos like postcards of the city's early days and a vintage domino set are tempting this local into buying a souvenir from her own hometown.

JAGUAR

Latin American fare and ceviche bar

3067 Grand Avenue (near Matilda Street) / +1 305 444 0216
jaguarhg.com/jaguarspot / Open daily

A few years ago, Jaguar was one of the few non-chain restaurants where a local could eat if they were "stranded" in the area. These days, it's flanked by gastronomic heavyweights such as LoKal (see pg 121) and 33 Kitchen. Still, Jaguar's long-standing reputation for delectable nosh allows it to continue to hold its own. If you like raw seafood, their ceviche spoon sampler is a good item to order on your first visit because it allows you to taste the different options before committing. I'm obsessed with ponzu sauce, so the ceviche nuevo, with its citrus and soy flavor profile, is a must-have. If that isn't your thing, consider the sandwiches, salads, casual corner (think quesadillas and tacos) and grill menus, all of which showcase the restaurant's culinary inspiration.

LE BOUCHON DU GROVE

Lyonnaise cuisine in a quaint bistro

3430 Main Highway (near Fuller Street) / +1 305 448 6060
lebouchondugrove.com / Open daily

The Grove is a prime weekend destination because of its café-lined streets that are ideal for brunch or a romantic dinner. While Lulu in the Grove and Green Street Café are most people's default, sometimes I'm not in the mood to wait 45 minutes for a table. Enter Le Bouchon du Grove, a tiny outfit only one block north of the two aforementioned dining spots. Its claim to fame is its ambiance, which, along with the rustic French décor, perfectly complements its cuisine. The space is tight and can get super packed, particularly for dinner, so I recommend only visiting with a small group – if not so you can fit comfortably, then so you have fewer people to battle for the warm, crusty French bread.

LOKAL

Mouthwatering goodness

RECOMMENDED BY **DIANNE RUBIN & GEOFFREY ANDERSON**
FOUNDERS OF MIAMIFOODPUG.COM

3190 Commodore Plaza (at Grand Avenue) / +1 305 442 3377
lokalmiami.com / Open daily

My friend Morgan knows Coconut Grove the way I know Miami Beach, so when she asked to go to LoKal for her birthday, I knew it had to be damn worthy. Her choice did not disappoint. If you're on a diet, steer clear of this carby, greasy heaven – you just don't come here to eat a salad. For those of you who aren't counting calories, then you absolutely need to try the grub here because you won't find burgers or sandwiches like these anywhere else. I'm talking about Miami-inspired recipes using grass-fed beef and locally sourced ingredients like guava jelly as well as melted Gruyère, candied bacon and even a seared doughnut bun. LoKal is food porn central and it is exceedingly good.

THE BARNACLE HISTORIC STATE PARK

Oldest Miami house in its original location

3485 Main Highway (near Via Abitare Way) / +1 305 442 6866
floridastateparks.org/thebarnacle / Closed Tuesday

Local history is punctuated by deadly tropical storms, such as the "Great Miami" hurricane of 1926 and Hurricane Andrew in 1992. Places that have survived through it all hold a certain type of wonder for me because they are few and far between in South Florida. This venue is especially amazing considering the boathouse on the property was destroyed in both storms; it's almost as if it was spared to serve some higher purpose – perhaps to remind us all of the challenges our city had to overcome to become what it is today. Nevertheless, this is a gorgeous bayfront property and a short walk from the Grove's eateries. Do yourself a favor and stop by while you're in the area. You can take a guided tour of the house and gardens or explore the property grounds on your own.

THE BOOKSTORE IN THE GROVE

Literary joint with heart

3390 Mary Street #166 (at Florida Avenue) / +1 305 443 2855
thebookstoreinthegrove.com / Open daily

The Bookstore in the Grove is a venue you can't help but like. The first time I walked in here was for a coffee with Morgan, and I ended up picking a novel that caught my eye. The girl at the register was extremely amped that I was buying the book because it was their book club selection for the month. I signed up for their mailing list, which has only made me love this place more. Recently, they've held a *Game of Thrones*-themed dinner, and when Vietnamese eatery Hy Vong had to leave their Little Havana digs due to sky-high rent, they let them hold a pop-up in their space. I can't wait to see what else they have up their sleeves.

Nine-acre, Southeast Asia-inspired garden

4013 Douglas Road (near Bay Breeze Avenue) / +1 305 442 7169
ntbg.org/gardens/kampong.php / Closed Sunday

I am not sure why or how, but I am obsessed with facets of Asian cultures, particularly those of East Asia. At the top of my bucket list are trips to Japan, Thailand, Indonesia and the Philippines, much like the trips that American botanist David Fairchild took with his wife, Marian, the daughter of Alexander Graham Bell. Fortunately for me – since I can't just jet off for months at a time – the plants and treasures that they collected throughout their travels made it back to their estate at The Kampong and give the garden its unique atmosphere. So, while a trip across the Pacific is not currently in the cards for me, a picnic and self-guided tour through The Kampong's stunning grounds does not make for a bad consolation prize.

soak up the sun

Explore the fabulous outdoors

COCONUT GROVE ORGANIC MARKET
3300 Grand Avenue (near Margaret Street; Coconut Grove), +1 305 238 7747 glaserorganicfarms.com/market.php, every Saturday

MATHESON HAMMOCK PARK
9610 Old Cutler Road (at Matheson Park; South Miami) +1 305 665 5475, miamidade.gov/parks/matheson-hammock.asp

SOUNDSCAPE PARK
400 17th Street (at Washington Avenue; Miami Beach), +1 305 673 3330, nws.edu/events-tickets/wallcast-concerts-and-park-events

SOUTH POINTE PARK
1 Washington Avenue (near Inlet Boulevard; Miami Beach), +1 305 673 7779 miamibeachfl.gov/parksandrecreation

THE RATHSKELLER
1330 Miller Drive (near San Amaro Drive; Coral Gables) +1 305 284 6310, ntbg.org/gardens/kampong.php closed Sunday and in summer

THE STANDARD SPA MIAMI BEACH
40 Island Avenue (near Century Lane; Miami Beach) +1 305 673 1717, standardhotels.com/miami/properties/miami-beach, open daily

SOUTH POINTE PARK

THE STANDARD SPA MIAMI BEACH

Building on the knowledge that Miami is coveted for its balmy climate, I wanted to curate for you a list of some of the city's most magnificent outdoor spots – the places that I depend on when I really need to blow someone away with the city's charm. At the top of that list is **South Pointe Park**. I love it not only because it boasts views of the Atlantic Ocean, Biscayne Bay, the Port of Miami and the downtown skyline, but because it's suitable for a wide range of activities, including surfing, paddleboarding and kiteboarding, with rentals available at nearby F1rst Surf Shop.

Right smack in the middle of South Beach is **Soundscape Park**, which is of most interest to me on Wednesday nights when I can post up with my lawn chair and a full picnic on the grass to enjoy a free movie screened on the wall of the New World Symphony building.

A few blocks northwest lies the more expensive but equally enjoyable experience of hanging out at **The Standard Spa Miami Beach** pool with awe-inspiring views of Biscayne Bay. The day pass grants you access to the spa's gym, relaxing hammam and ultra-hip pool deck where you can tan, nosh on healthy fare, or listen to underwater music as you take a dip.

If you're looking to escape the Beach, the **Coconut Grove Organic Market** on Saturdays is a fun activity to keep you occupied as you navigate rows upon rows of food and knick-knack vendors. Don't want to walk? I feel ya. In that case, the gliders along the shores of the University of Miami's Lake Osceola at **The Rathskeller** are what you need, along with a pitcher of ice-cold beer and some bar bites to keep you company.

Alternatively, if you prefer to be active, you can lounge by the uncrowded atoll beach, book a snorkeling tour, rent a kayak or paddleboard, or go hiking along the mangrove trails of nearby **Matheson Hammock Park**. Once the activity builds your appetite, the Red Fish Grill, tucked in the park, is a local's power move for lunch and dinner.

MATHESON HAMMOCK PARK